GLENCOE LANGUAGE ARTS

VOCABULARY POWER

GRADE 9

Glencoe McGraw-Hill

New York, New York   Columbus, Ohio   Woodland Hills, California   Peoria, Illinois

To the Student

This *Vocabulary Power* workbook gives you the practice you need to expand your vocabulary and improve your ability to understand what you read. Each lesson focuses on a single vocabulary concept or on a theme that ties together the list of words in the Word Bank. You then have several opportunities to learn the words by completing exercises on definitions, context clues, and word parts.

You can keep track of your own progress and achievement in vocabulary study by using the Student Progress Chart, which appears on page v. With your teacher's help, you can score your work on any lesson or test. After you know your score, use the Scoring Scale on pages vi–vii to figure your percentage. Then mark your score (or percentage correct) on the Student Progress Chart. Share your Progress Chart with your parents or guardians as your teacher directs.

Glencoe/McGraw-Hill

A Division of The **McGraw-Hill** Companies

Send all inquiries to:
Glencoe/McGraw-Hill
8787 Orion Place
Columbus, Ohio 43240

ISBN 0-07-826230-5

Printed in the United States of America

11 12 13 024 10 09

CONTENTS

Student Progress Chart v
Scoring Scale vi

Unit 1
Lesson 1   Using Context Clues 1
Lesson 2   The Prefix *im-* 3
Lesson 3   Word Families 5
Lesson 4   Using Reference Skills—Using a Dictionary: Etymology 7
Review 8
Test 9

Unit 2
Lesson 5   Using Synonyms 11
Lesson 6   Prefixes Meaning "not" 13
Lesson 7   Words Formed from the Root *vidēre* 15
Lesson 8   Using Reference Skills—Using a Thesaurus: Synonyms 17
Review 18
Test 19

Unit 3
Lesson 9   Using Synonyms 21
Lesson 10   The Latin Root *mille* 23
Lesson 11   The Suffix *-ous* 25
Lesson 12   Using Reading Skills—Drawing Inferences 27
Review 28
Test 29

Unit 4
Lesson 13   Usage 31
Lesson 14   Using Context Clues 33
Lesson 15   The Latin Root *crux* 35
Review 37
Test 38

Unit 5
Lesson 16   Using Synonyms 40
Lesson 17   The Prefix *ex-* 42
Lesson 18   The Greek Roots *hydr, hydro* 44
Lesson 19   Using Reading Skills—Word Parts 46
Review 47
Test 48

Unit 6
Lesson 20   Using Context Clues 50
Lesson 21   Using Synonyms 52
Lesson 22   The Word Roots *viv, vit, vita* 54
Lesson 23   Using Reading Skills—Clarifying Meaning 56
Review 57
Test 58

Unit 7

Lesson 24   Usage 60
Lesson 25   Words Related to Writing 62
Lesson 26   The Latin Roots *dic/dict* and *claim/clam* 64
Lesson 27   Using Reference Skills—Using a Dictionary: Multiple-Meaning Words 66
Review 67
Test 68

Unit 8

Lesson 28   Using Synonyms 70
Lesson 29   The Suffix *-ist* 72
Lesson 30   The Word Root *spir* 74
Lesson 31   Using Reading Skills—Context Clues 76
Review 77
Test 78

Unit 9

Lesson 32   Using Synonyms 80
Lesson 33   Compound Words 82
Lesson 34   The Suffixes *-able* and *-ible* 84
Review 86
Test 87

Unit 10

Lesson 35   Using Synonyms 89
Lesson 36   Using Context Clues 91
Lesson 37   Prefixes That Tell When 93
Lesson 38   Using Reading Skills—Connotation and Denotation 95
Review 96
Test 97

Unit 11

Lesson 39   Using Context Clues 99
Lesson 40   The Latin Roots *cede, ceed, cess* 101
Lesson 41   The Prefixes *circu-, circum-,* and *trans-* 103
Lesson 42   Using Reference Skills—Using a Thesaurus: Antonyms 105
Review 106
Test 107

Unit 12

Lesson 43   Using Synonyms 109
Lesson 44   Words from Technology 111
Lesson 45   Prefixes That Tell Where 113
Lesson 46   Using Test-Taking Skills—Analogies 115
Review 116
Test 117

Pronunciation Guide 119

STUDENT PROGRESS CHART

Fill in the chart below with your scores, using the scoring scale on the next page.

Name: _____

	Lesson	Unit Review	Unit Test
1			
2			
3			
4			
Review			
Test			
5			
6			
7			
8			
Review			
Test			
9			
10			
11			
12			
Review			
Test			
13			
14			
15			
Review			
Test			
16			
17			
18			
19			
Review			
Test			
20			
21			
22			
23			
Review			
Test			
24			
25			
26			
27			
Review			
Test			
28			
29			
30			
31			
Review			
Test			
32			
33			
34			
Review			
Test			
35			
36			
37			
38			
Review			
Test			
39			
40			
41			
42			
Review			
Test			
43			
44			
45			
46			
Review			
Test			

SCORING SCALE

Use this scale to find your score. Line up the number of items with the number correct. For example, if 15 out of 16 items are correct, the score is 93.7 percent (see grayed area).

Number Correct

Number of Items

	1	2	3	4	5	6	7	8	9	10	11	12	13	14	15	16	17	18	19	20
1	100																			
2	50	100																		
3	33.3	66.7	100																	
4	25	50	75	100																
5	20	40	60	80	100															
6	16.7	33.3	50	66.7	83.3	100														
7	14.3	28.6	42.9	57.1	71.4	85.7	100													
8	12.5	25	37.5	50	62.5	75	87.5	100												
9	11.1	22.2	33.3	44.4	55.6	66.7	77.8	88.9	100											
10	10	20	30	40	50	60	70	80	90	100										
11	9.1	18.1	27.2	36.3	45.4	54.5	63.6	72.7	81.8	90.9	100									
12	8.3	16.7	25	33.3	41.7	50	58.3	66.7	75	83.3	91.7	100								
13	7.7	15.3	23.1	30.8	38.5	46.1	53.8	61.5	69.2	76.9	84.6	92.3	100							
14	7.1	14.3	21.4	28.6	35.7	42.8	50	57.1	64.3	71.4	78.5	85.7	92.8	100						
15	6.7	13.3	20	26.7	33.3	40	46.6	53.3	60	66.7	73.3	80	86.7	93.3	100					
16	6.3	12.5	18.8	25	31.2	37.5	43.7	50	56.2	62.5	68.7	75	81.2	87.5	93.7	100				
17	5.9	11.8	17.6	23.5	29.4	35.3	41.2	47	52.9	58.8	64.7	70.6	76.5	82.3	88.2	94.1	100			
18	5.6	11.1	16.7	22.2	27.8	33.3	38.9	44.4	50	55.5	61.1	66.7	72.2	77.8	83.3	88.9	94.4	100		
19	5.3	10.5	15.8	21	26.3	31.6	36.8	42.1	47.4	52.6	57.9	63.1	68.4	73.7	78.9	84.2	89.4	94.7	100	
20	5	10	15	20	25	30	35	40	45	50	55	60	65	70	75	80	85	90	95	100
21	4.8	9.5	14.3	19	23.8	28.6	33.3	38.1	42.8	47.6	52.3	57.1	61.9	66.7	71.4	76.1	80.9	85.7	90.5	95.2
22	4.5	9.1	13.7	18.2	22.7	27.3	31.8	36.4	40.9	45.4	50	54.5	59.1	63.6	68.1	72.7	77.2	81.8	86.4	90.9
23	4.3	8.7	13	17.4	21.7	26.1	30.4	34.8	39.1	43.5	47.8	52.1	56.5	60.8	65.2	69.5	73.9	78.3	82.6	86.9
24	4.2	8.3	12.5	16.7	20.8	25	29.2	33.3	37.5	41.7	45.8	50	54.2	58.3	62.5	66.7	70.8	75	79.1	83.3
25	4	8	12	16	20	24	28	32	36	40	44	48	52	56	60	64	68	72	76	80
26	3.8	7.7	11.5	15.4	19.2	23.1	26.9	30.8	34.6	38.5	42.3	46.2	50	53.8	57.7	61.5	65.4	69.2	73.1	76.9
27	3.7	7.4	11.1	14.8	18.5	22.2	25.9	29.6	33.3	37	40.7	44.4	48.1	51.9	55.6	59.2	63	66.7	70.4	74.1
28	3.6	7.1	10.7	14.3	17.9	21.4	25	28.6	32.1	35.7	39.3	42.9	46.4	50	53.6	57.1	60.7	64.3	67.9	71.4
29	3.4	6.9	10.3	13.8	17.2	20.7	24.1	27.6	31	34.5	37.9	41.4	44.8	48.3	51.7	55.2	58.6	62.1	65.5	69
30	3.3	6.7	10	13.3	16.7	20	23.3	26.7	30	33.3	36.7	40	43.3	46.7	50	53.3	56.7	60	63.3	66.7
31	3.2	6.5	9.7	13	16.1	19.3	22.6	25.8	29	32.2	35.4	38.7	41.9	45.1	48.3	51.6	54.8	58	61.2	64.5
32	3.1	6.3	9.4	12.5	15.6	18.8	21.9	25	28.1	31.3	34.4	37.5	40.6	43.8	46.9	50	53.1	56.2	59.4	62.5
33	3	6	9	12.1	15.1	18.1	21.2	24.2	27.2	30.3	33	36.3	39.3	42.4	45.4	48.4	51.5	54.5	57.5	60.6
34	2.9	5.9	8.8	11.8	14.7	17.6	20.6	23.5	26.5	29.4	32.4	35.3	38.2	41.2	44.1	47.1	50	52.9	55.9	58.8
35	2.9	5.7	8.6	11.4	14.3	17.1	20	22.9	25.7	28.6	31.4	34.3	37.1	40	42.9	45.7	48.6	51.4	54.3	57.1
36	2.8	5.6	8.3	11.1	13.9	16.7	19.4	22.2	25	27.8	30.6	33.3	36.1	38.9	41.7	44.4	47.2	50	52.7	55.6
37	2.7	5.4	8.1	10.8	13.5	16.2	18.9	21.6	24.3	27	29.7	32.4	35.1	37.8	40.5	43.2	45.9	48.6	51.4	54
38	2.6	5.3	7.9	10.5	13.2	15.8	18.4	21.1	23.7	26.3	28.9	31.6	34.2	36.8	39.5	42.1	44.7	47.4	50	52.6
39	2.6	5.2	7.7	10.3	12.8	15.4	17.9	20.5	23.1	25.6	28.2	30.8	33.3	35.9	38.5	41	43.6	46.2	48.7	51.3
40	2.5	5	7.5	10	12.5	15	17.5	20	22.5	25	27.5	30	32.5	35	37.5	40	42.5	45	47.5	50

Number Correct

Number of Items

	21	22	23	24	25	26	27	28	29	30	31	32	33	34	35	36	37	38	39	40
1																				
2																				
3																				
4																				
5																				
6																				
7																				
8																				
9																				
10																				
11																				
12																				
13																				
14																				
15																				
16																				
17																				
18																				
19																				
20																				
21	100																			
22	95.4	100																		
23	91.3	95.6	100																	
24	87.5	91.6	95.8	100																
25	84	88	92	96	100															
26	80.8	84.6	88.5	92.3	96.2	100														
27	77.8	81.5	85.2	88.9	92.6	96.3	100													
28	75	78.6	82.1	85.7	89.3	92.9	96.4	100												
29	72.4	75.9	79.3	82.8	86.2	89.7	93.1	96.6	100											
30	70	73.3	76.7	80	83.3	86.7	90	93.3	96.7	100										
31	67.7	70.9	74.2	77.4	80.6	83.9	87.1	90.3	93.5	96.8	100									
32	65.6	68.8	71.9	75	78.1	81.2	84.4	87.5	90.6	93.8	96.9	100								
33	63.6	66.7	69.7	72.7	75.8	78.8	81.8	84.8	87.8	90.9	93.9	96.9	100							
34	61.8	64.7	67.6	70.6	73.5	76.5	79.4	82.4	85.3	88.2	91.2	94.1	97.1	100						
35	60	62.9	65.7	68.6	71.4	74.3	77.1	80	82.9	85.7	88.6	91.4	94.4	97.1	100					
36	58.3	61.1	63.8	66.7	69.4	72.2	75	77.8	80.6	83.3	86.1	88.9	91.7	94.4	97.2	100				
37	56.8	59.5	62.2	64.9	67.6	70.3	72.9	75.7	78.4	81.1	83.8	86.5	89.2	91.9	94.6	97.3	100			
38	55.3	57.9	60.5	63.2	65.8	68.4	71.1	73.7	76.3	78.9	81.6	84.2	86.8	89.5	92.1	94.7	97.3	100		
39	53.8	56.4	58.9	61.5	64.1	66.7	69.2	71.8	74.4	76.9	79.5	82.1	84.6	87.2	89.7	92.3	94.9	97.4	100	
40	52.5	55	57.5	60	62.5	65	67.5	70	72.5	75	77.5	80	82.5	85	87.5	90	92.5	95	97.5	100

Vocabulary Power

Lesson 1   Using Context Clues

How you react when faced with physical or emotional danger can often mean the difference between life and death. The words in this lesson relate to matters of life and death.

Word List

commemorate	eulogy	predator	sustenance
dire	immortality	quarry	vital
epitaph	longevity		

EXERCISE A   Context Clues

When you come across an unfamiliar word while reading, you can often use clues from the "context," the sentence or paragraph in which it appears, to figure out the word's meaning. For each sentence below use context clues to determine the meaning of the boldfaced vocabulary word. Write your definition of the word. Then, look up the word and write the dictionary definition.

1. To remember those who died, we will build a monument to **commemorate** them.

   My definition _____

   Dictionary definition _____

2. In the **eulogy** at his grandmother's funeral, Kimo spoke of all the wonderful things he remembered about her.

   My definition _____

   Dictionary definition _____

3. From paintings that show whales attacking ships, you might not realize that a whale's favorite **quarry** is giant squid.

   My definition _____

   Dictionary definition _____

4. Many refugees would die unless they received **vital** supplies such as food and medicine.

   My definition _____

   Dictionary definition _____

5. Bananas provided **sustenance** for the sailors who were shipwrecked on the island.

   My definition _____

   Dictionary definition _____

6. A **dire** forecast on the radio prompted everyone to leave the hurricane area immediately.

   My definition _____

   Dictionary definition _____

Vocabulary Power continued

7. People have long dreamed of achieving **immortality,** but would it really be good to live forever?

   My definition _____

   Dictionary definition _____

8. The words of the **epitaph** carved into the tombstone had worn away.

   My definition _____

   Dictionary definition _____

9. Most plants are not **predators,** but the Venus's-flytrap captures and eats insects.

   My definition _____

   Dictionary definition _____

10. **Longevity** runs in Rudy's family; all four of his grandparents have lived to ninety years of age.

    My definition _____

    Dictionary definition _____

EXERCISE B Usage
Circle the letter of the answer that best completes each sentence.

1. A **eulogy** probably would *not* contain _____.
   - **a.** stories about good things the person had done
   - **b.** an excerpt from a poem the person had written
   - **c.** a detailed description of how the person died
   - **d.** reasons why the person will be remembered

2. An example of **sustenance** is _____.
   - **a.** a bouquet of flowers
   - **b.** a loaf of bread
   - **c.** movies on videotape
   - **d.** toothpaste

3. A person's **epitaph** would probably contain _____.
   - **a.** the person's street address
   - **b.** photographs from a recent vacation
   - **c.** the person's baseball card collection
   - **d.** the person's birth date

4. You could **commemorate** someone by _____.
   - **a.** ignoring all of the person's faults
   - **b.** taking the person out for lunch
   - **c.** telling the person why you like him or her
   - **d.** dedicating a building in the person's honor

5. A **predator** would probably not be very successful if it _____.
   - **a.** was much weaker than its prey
   - **b.** could move very fast
   - **c.** was able to hide itself and remain very still
   - **d.** had large and powerful jaws

Vocabulary Power

Lesson 2   The Prefix *im-*

A prefix is a syllable placed before a root or base word to change or add to its meaning. Some prefixes have more than one meaning. For example, the prefix *im-* can mean "not," or it can mean "in," "within," or "into." The vocabulary words in this lesson have the prefix *im-* and are related to the theme of justice.

Word List

immaterial	imperceptible	impervious	imprint
impartial	impersonate	implausible	imprison
impenitent	imperturbable		

EXERCISE A   Synonyms

Synonyms are words with similar meanings. Each boldfaced vocabulary word is paired with a synonym whose meaning you probably know. Brainstorm other words related to the meaning of the synonym and write your ideas on the line provided. Then, look up the vocabulary word in a dictionary and write its meaning.

1. **impartial** : fair _____

   Dictionary definition _____

2. **imprint** : impress _____

   Dictionary definition _____

3. **imperceptible** : undetectable _____

   Dictionary definition _____

4. **immaterial** : unimportant _____

   Dictionary definition _____

5. **imperturbable** : calm _____

   Dictionary definition _____

6. **imprison** : confine _____

   Dictionary definition _____

7. **impenitent** : shameless _____

   Dictionary definition _____

8. **impersonate** : imitate _____

   Dictionary definition _____

9. **implausible** : unbelievable _____

   Dictionary definition _____

10. **impervious** : unchanging _____

    Dictionary definition _____

Vocabulary Power *continued*

EXERCISE B Base Words

Write the meaning of the base word in each word below. Then, write the meaning of the word. Write a sentence for each word.

1. impersonate _____

_____

2. imperturbable _____

_____

3. imprint _____

_____

4. imprison _____

_____

5. impervious _____

_____

EXERCISE C Sentence Completion

Circle the word in each set of parentheses that best completes the sentence.

1. It is against the law to (imprison, impersonate, imprint) a police officer.

2. The judge's (immaterial, impenitent, imperturbable) personality prevented him from becoming easily upset during the trial.

3. The slight twitching of the defendant's face was (imperceptible, impartial, impervious) to the jurors.

4. The lawyer tried to make the defendant contradict himself, but the man was (immaterial, impenitent, impervious) to her tactics.

5. The defendant smiled as she admitted her guilt, showing that she was (imperceptible, implausible, impenitent).

EXERCISE D Headlines

Imagine that you are a newspaper reporter covering the "trial of the century"–a court case that has everyone in the country glued to the radio and television. On a separate sheet of paper, write several newspaper headlines using five of the vocabulary words to describe what is happening in this imaginary trial.

Vocabulary Power

Lesson 3 Word Families

A word family is made up of words that have a common origin or root. Many words in the English language trace their roots to Greek or Latin. The vocabulary words in this lesson belong to two Latin word families–*claudere,* meaning "to close," and *strictus,* meaning "to bind." All of the vocabulary words are related to the theme of facing limitations.

> ### Word List
>
> | | | | |
> |---|---|---|---|
> | cloister | enclosure | preclude | strain |
> | close | exclude | restrict | stricture |
> | constricting | exclusion | | |

EXERCISE A Context Clues

For each sentence below, use context clues to determine the meaning of the boldfaced vocabulary word. Write your definition of the word. Then, look up the word in a dictionary and write the definition.

1. The jeans Joel tried on were **constricting,** so he asked for a larger size.

   My definition _____

   Dictionary definition _____

2. I try to **restrict** my intake of candy to one chocolate bar per week.

   My definition _____

   Dictionary definition _____

3. Some students disliked the clothing **stricture** and wanted to dress however they pleased.

   My definition _____

   Dictionary definition _____

4. I will need to **strain** to run faster than the other runners in the race.

   My definition _____

   Dictionary definition _____

5. To **preclude** any problems underwater, the diver carefully checked his scuba equipment.

   My definition _____

   Dictionary definition _____

6. To aid the firefighters, police decided to **close** the streets around the burning building.

   My definition _____

   Dictionary definition _____

7. Scientists are often as reclusive as monks in a **cloister** when they are close to a breakthrough in their research.

   My definition _____

   Dictionary definition _____

Vocabulary Power *continued*

8. We built a fence around our garden, hoping that animals would not get into the **enclosure.**

   My definition _____

   Dictionary definition _____

9. Theaters must **exclude** children under seventeen years of age from R-rated movies.

   My definition _____

   Dictionary definition _____

10. Jean-Pierre could not understand the **exclusion** of pets from American restaurants; in Paris he always took

    his dog along when he went to a café.

    My definition _____

    Dictionary definition _____

EXERCISE B   Multiple-Meaning Words

Many words in English have more than one meaning. Each meaning, however, is based on the meaning of the word root. The word *close,* **for example, is from the Latin root** *claudere,* **meaning "to close." A dictionary entry for** *close* **lists many different meanings, but all of them are related to the root meaning "to close." Use a dictionary to help you write the precise definition of** *close* **as it is used in each sentence below.**

1. It is customary for banks to **close** on Thanksgiving Day.

   Definition _____

2. Make sure to **close** the bag or the chips will become stale.

   Definition _____

3. I wanted to **close** the conversation, but my little sister kept asking questions.

   Definition _____

4. Please **close** and lock the door on your way out.

   Definition _____

5. The state will **close** the beach until it is safe for people to swim.

   Definition _____

Vocabulary Power

Lesson 4   Using Reference Skills
Using a Dictionary: Etymology

Many words in the English language are derived from words in other languages. Most dictionaries give information about a word's etymology, or origin, at the beginning or end of an entry. For example, if you looked up the word *scruple,* you might find the following information.

> **scruple,** *fr.* L *scrupulus* cause of mental discomfort, dim. of *scrupus* sharp stone

In this case, the meaning of the Latin word *scrupus,* "sharp stone," evolved to mean a moral principle that makes a person hesitate before acting. Just as having a stone lodged painfully in your shoe would prevent you from walking, a scruple can prevent you from doing something that you know is wrong. Note that each dictionary uses a slightly different style for its word origin notes. A key to interpreting the notes appears at the beginning of the dictionary.

EXERCISE A

Use a dictionary to find the etymology of each word below. Write the originating language, the word root, and the meaning of each root.

1. commemorate _____
2. dolphin _____
3. fiddle _____
4. quay _____
5. zoology _____
6. fortitude _____
7. fervent _____
8. potato _____
9. giraffe _____
10. kayak _____

EXERCISE B

Use your dictionary skills to solve a word origins puzzle. All of the words—except one—are derived from the same root. Read the following words: *maritime, marina, marinate, maroon, marinara, marine, mariner.* Which one does not belong?

_____

What is the common root of the other words? What does it mean? From what language is it?

_____
_____

Vocabulary Power

Review: Unit 1

EXERCISE

Circle the word in each set of parentheses that best completes the sentence.

1. After the battle ended, Lieutenant Shull sadly buried his fallen friend and carved an (exclusion, epitaph, immortality) into a nearby tree.

2. My puppy finds his (cloister, quarry, enclosure) in the backyard too (vital, constricting, imperceptible), so he's always trying to escape.

3. Some of the crew members wondered whether the director had made an (impartial, implausible, immaterial) decision when she gave her best friend the lead role in the play.

4. Despite the (impervious, dire, vital) forecast, the "blizzard" yielded less than an inch of snow.

5. Insects are not known for their (longevity, epitaph, stricture), but the female termite can live up to fifty years.

6. Each year on this date, my parents dress up like a bride and groom to (impersonate, preclude, commemorate) their wedding day.

7. From where she stood in the (cloister, stricture, eulogy), Jane looked out on the courtyard and enjoyed the (dire, implausible, imperturbable) calm.

8. Sean spent some extra time studying his geometry in order to (imprint, imprison, preclude) failure on the test.

9. Playing on a well-tuned piano is (impervious, immaterial, impenitent) if you haven't practiced the song.

10. The comedian was trying to (commemorate, exclude, impersonate) the president, but he didn't sound or act anything like him.

11. Brad had a hard time limiting his (eulogy, longevity, enclosure) to fifteen minutes because his grandfather had so many fine qualities.

12. The (stricture, cloister, sustenance) Sandy placed on her dog was to prevent him from chewing her shoes.

13. An experienced detective can find subtle clues that would be (impartial, implausible, imperceptible) to ordinary people.

14. The shark saw its (predator, quarry, cloister) and moved in for the kill.

15. I can't imagine why Victoria would (exclude, preclude, imprint) Amy from her birthday party; I thought they were good friends.

Vocabulary Power

Test: Unit 1

PART A

For each boldfaced word, circle the letter of the word that is most nearly *opposite* in meaning.

1. sustenance
   a. life   b. illness   c. health   d. poison

2. commemorate
   a. rejoice   b. forget   c. recall   d. release

3. immortality
   a. courage   b. faith   c. death   d. kindness

4. constricting
   a. freeing   b. tightening   c. stopping   d. moving

5. exclude
   a. destroy   b. include   c. preclude   d. expel

6. impartial
   a. judgmental   b. loving   c. excited   d. unfair

7. imperceptible
   a. small   b. sneaky   c. visible   d. enormous

8. vital
   a. crucial   b. unimportant   c. durable   d. strong

9. impenitent
   a. ashamed   b. proud   c. friendly   d. harsh

10. implausible
    a. amazing   b. forgettable   c. open   d. believable

PART B

Circle the letter of the word that best completes each sentence.

1. Rose signed the petition for the _____ of jet skis from the lake because she disliked the noise pollution.
   a. inclusion   b. immortality   c. sustenance   d. exclusion

2. The gravestone was surrounded by so many flowers that it was impossible to read the _____.
   a. eulogy   b. epitaph   c. stricture   d. enclosure

3. I wish that my running shoes had greater _____; I seem to need a new pair every six months.
   a. longevity   b. exclusion   c. sustenance   d. stricture

Vocabulary Power *continued*

4. Mother built a tall fence to serve as a(n) _____ for the vegetable garden.
   a. enclosure   **b.** exclusion   **c.** epitaph   **d.** cloister

5. One small mistake can have _____ consequences for a rock climber.
   a. immaterial   **b.** implausible   **c.** dire   **d.** imperturbable

6. If you truly want to strive for a goal, you must be _____ to opinions of people who don't think you can do it.
   a. imperceptible   **b.** impenitent   **c.** impartial   **d.** impervious

7. Jack's argument was not very strong; most of his facts were _____ to the point he was trying to make.
   a. vital   **b.** immaterial   **c.** constricting   **d.** dire

8. In her _____, Debbie told stories about her great-uncle that showed how funny, wise, and unselfish he was.
   a. cloister   **b.** epitaph   **c.** eulogy   **d.** enclosure

9. After the long ceremony, the wedding guests rushed toward the food like beasts of prey closing in on their _____.
   a. quarry   **b.** enclosure   **c.** predator   **d.** cloister

10. Before leaving on their trip, Jennifer's parents did everything they could to _____ a big party at their house while they were gone.
    a. close   **b.** strain   **c.** imprint   **d.** preclude

PART C

Circle the letter of the best answer to each question.

1. If you were looking at a cloister, where would you be?
   a. at the top of a mountain   **c.** in a monastery
   b. in a courtroom   **d.** in a candy factory

2. What is an example of a predator?
   a. a tomato   **c.** a mouse
   b. a computer   **d.** a hawk

3. What is another word for a stricture?
   a. limit   **c.** jury
   b. gravestone   **d.** church

4. What might you use to impersonate someone?
   a. a statue of the person   **c.** a videotape of the person
   b. your voice and facial expressions   **d.** a cake and party decorations

5. How would an imperturbable person react to an annoying situation?
   a. by getting angry   **c.** by telling everyone what to do
   b. by remaining calm   **d.** by running away

   Vocabulary Power

Vocabulary Power

Lesson 5   Using Synonyms

Void, abyss, chasm—all these words suggest a hole, nothingness, something missing. Filling a void in one's life often leads to a fulfillment of one's dreams. The words in this list relate to voids.

Word List

avocation	fortuitous	privation	renaissance
bereft	introspection	provisional	solace
epiphany	melancholy		

EXERCISE A   Synonyms

Each boldfaced word below is paired with a synonym whose meaning you probably know. Brainstorm other words related to the meaning of the synonym and write your ideas on the line provided. Then, look up the vocabulary word in a dictionary and write its meaning.

1. **privation** : lack _____

   Dictionary definition _____

2. **solace** : comfort _____

   Dictionary definition _____

3. **introspection** : self-examination _____

   Dictionary definition _____

4. **provisional** : temporary _____

   Dictionary definition _____

5. **bereft** : deprived _____

   Dictionary definition _____

6. **epiphany** : insight _____

   Dictionary definition _____

7. **fortuitous** : accidental _____

   Dictionary definition _____

8. **melancholy** : sadness _____

   Dictionary definition _____

9. **avocation** : hobby _____

   Dictionary definition _____

10. **renaissance** : rebirth _____

    Dictionary definition _____

Vocabulary Power *continued*

EXERCISE B Usage

Circle the word in each set of parentheses that best completes the sentence.

1. The city council created a (bereft, provisional, fortuitous) ordinance to last until election time.

2. Her kind words provided (privation, introspection, solace) after my mother's death.

3. Most people who enjoy surfing do it as a(n) (avocation, epiphany, renaissance), but a few lucky ones can make careers of it.

4. (Solace, Introspection, Epiphany) is a good way to figure out what you want from life, but it can be unwise to spend too much time looking inward.

5. Who would have expected bell-bottom pants to experience a fashion (solace, renaissance, epiphany) after twenty-five years?

EXERCISE C Multiple-Meaning Words

Some words have several related definitions listed within a single dictionary entry. To explore the multiple meanings of words in the vocabulary list, select the expression that correctly completes each statement below. Use a dictionary, if necessary.

1. **Bereft** can mean "deprived of or lacking something," but it can also mean _____.
   a. feeling very embarrassed
   b. being of less than average height
   c. being lost at sea
   d. suffering the loss of a loved one

2. **Epiphany** can mean "a sudden insight or realization about an underlying truth," or it can mean _____.
   a. the part of a symphony when the resolution becomes clear
   b. an experience in which a divine being reveals itself plainly
   c. a kind of glass that refracts light into brilliant colors
   d. a mystery novel in which the crime is solved very suddenly at the end

3. **Fortuitous** can mean "happening purely by accident" or _____.
   a. causing an unexpected disaster
   b. funny in an ironic way
   c. forcing someone to look at a problem in a new way
   d. lucky or fortunate

4. **Melancholy** can have the meaning "sadness or gloom," but it can also mean _____.
   a. deep thought or reflection
   b. a disease of the skin
   c. feeling someone else's pain
   d. recovering from a severe shock or unpleasant surprise

EXERCISE D Plot Summary

Imagine that you have the chance to pitch an idea for a new movie that shows how people fill voids in their lives. The story can be funny, inspiring, tragic—whatever you like. On a separate sheet of paper, write a brief summary of the plot of your movie, using at least five of the vocabulary words.

Vocabulary Power

Lesson 6   Prefixes Meaning "not"

In English there are several prefixes—word parts attached to the beginning of a word—that add the meaning "not." These prefixes, which include *dis-, non-, im-, in-, ir-,* and *un-,* change the meaning of the base word to its opposite. The vocabulary words in this lesson begin with prefixes meaning "not" and are related to the theme of filling a void.

Word List

disconsolate	intractable	nonconformist	unsavory
disingenuous	irresolute	unpretentious	unscrupulous
impassive	irresponsible		

EXERCISE A   Context Clues

For each sentence below, use context clues, or clues from the surrounding text, to determine the meaning of the boldfaced vocabulary word. Write your definition of the word. Then, look up the word in a dictionary and write its definition.

1. Preparing to play a character who was **disconsolate**, the actor recalled how he felt that he would never be happy again after his father died.

   My definition _____

   Dictionary definition _____

2. The mother in this play is completely **unpretentious,** while her daughter puts on airs and acts like a snob.

   My definition _____

   Dictionary definition _____

3. The actress showed that her character was **disingenuous** by making her eye twitch slightly whenever the character was being dishonest or sneaky.

   My definition _____

   Dictionary definition _____

4. The play had a cast of many **unscrupulous** characters, so the person with moral principles stood out conspicuously.

   My definition _____

   Dictionary definition _____

5. Vanessa is very **irresponsible;** she had to throw out four plants that she forgot to water.

   My definition _____

   Dictionary definition _____

6. Do you find it more difficult to portray an **impassive** character or an emotional one?

   My definition _____

   Dictionary definition _____

Vocabulary Power *continued*

7. The **nonconformist** in the play refuses to dress like his friends and is not interested in having a job that will make him rich.

My definition _____

Dictionary definition _____

8. Many characters are **irresolute;** they can't decide who they're in love with from one act to the next.

My definition _____

Dictionary definition _____

9. Many actors love to play **unsavory** characters because they get to act out disagreeable qualities.

My definition _____

Dictionary definition _____

10. The young heroine of this play is completely **intractable** and will not do anything her parents ask of her.

My definition _____

Dictionary definition _____

EXERCISE B Analogies

Analogies show relationships between things or ideas. For example, in the analogy *finger : hand :: toe : foot,* the relationship in each pair of words is "part to whole." A *finger* is part of a whole *hand,* as a *toe* is part of a whole *foot.* Complete each analogy below by determining the relationship between the first pair of words. Then, choose the letter of the word that creates the same relationship in the second pair.

1. cheerful : gloomy :: snobbish : _____
   a. unpretentious   b. disconsolate   c. impassive   d. irresponsible

2. reliable : untrustworthy :: decisive : _____
   a. nonconformist   b. intractable   c. irresolute   d. unsavory

3. emotional : impassive :: moral : _____
   a. intractable   b. unscrupulous   c. unpretentious   d. irresolute

4. trustworthy : dishonest :: controlled : _____
   a. intractable   b. unsavory   c. disconsolate   d. unpretentious

5. steady : calm :: disagreeable : _____
   a. disingenuous   b. irresponsible   c. nonconformist   d. unsavory

Vocabulary Power

Vocabulary Power

Lesson 7   Words Formed from the Root *vidēre*

A large family of words in English is derived from the Latin root *vidēre,* which means "to see." Study the list of vocabulary words to find those that you already know. How do the meanings of these words relate to seeing?

Word List

evident	video	vision	vista
provident	visage	visitation	visualize
supervise	visible		

EXERCISE A   Context Clues

Read each sentence below and use context clues to determine the meaning of the boldfaced vocabulary word. Write your definition of the word. Then, look up the word and write the dictionary definition that fits the sentence.

1. Wendy had heard radio reports about the tornado, but the **video** images on television showed the full extent of the damage.

   My definition _____

   Dictionary definition _____

2. The glistening dark eyes of the old man's **visage** suggested a lifetime of experience and wisdom.

   My definition _____

   Dictionary definition _____

3. Derek was honored by a **visitation** from one of the tribal elders, who came to discuss plans for preserving the ancestral forest.

   My definition _____

   Dictionary definition _____

4. The Rocky Mountains are so tall that they are **visible** for miles.

   My definition _____

   Dictionary definition _____

5. Many athletes find it helpful before a game to **visualize** themselves giving their best performance.

   My definition _____

   Dictionary definition _____

6. Serena was amazed at how much her new eyeglasses improved her **vision.**

   My definition _____

   Dictionary definition _____

Vocabulary Power *continued*

7. The summer internship at the software company opened the **vista** of a career in computer programming.

   My definition _____

   Dictionary definition _____

8. That he was home from college was **evident** when I saw the pile of dirty dishes in the kitchen sink.

   My definition _____

   Dictionary definition _____

9. **Provident** planning ensures that you'll have enough money for retirement in the future.

   My definition _____

   Dictionary definition _____

10. An adult should **supervise** small children while they use tools such as scissors.

    My definition _____

    Dictionary definition _____

EXERCISE B Matching

Write the vocabulary word that best matches the clue or question.

1. Eyeglasses help improve this faculty.

   _____

2. If all the data in a science experiment pointed to a certain conclusion, how would you describe this conclusion?

   _____

3. When someone comes to see you, it's called this.

   _____

4. You're in a clothing store and a certain sweater catches your eye. What can you do to imagine how it would look on you?

   _____

5. Through a clearing in the thick woods, you see a vast expanse of farmland.

   _____

6. A person who prepares for the future is this.

   _____

7. You see this kind of image each time you turn on your television.

   _____

8. A person's emotions are often expressed here.

   _____

Vocabulary Power

Lesson 8   Using Reference Skills
Using a Thesaurus: Synonyms

A thesaurus is a reference book that groups words into families of synonyms, or words and phrases with similar meanings. Some thesauruses are set up alphabetically, so all you have to do is look up the word to find the list of synonyms. Others require you to find the word in an index and choose the synonym that has the meaning you want from a short list. Here's a sample index entry that you might find for the word *pandemonium:*

pandemonium

noise 53.3

turbulence 671.2

Let's say that *noise* is closest to the meaning you want. Next, you would find the category numbered 53.3 in the main section of the thesaurus. There you would find a long list of synonyms, including *blast, racket, din, clamor, uproar, rattle, roar, thunder, crash, brouhaha, hubbub, brawl,* and *commotion.* Take your pick!

EXERCISE

Choose the word from the list that could replace the boldfaced word in each sentence. Use a thesaurus as a resource.

astonished	**timorous**	**vengeful**
irreverent	**unorthodox**	**watchful**

1. The girl was **amazed** and stared in wonder as the ugly toad was transformed into a handsome prince.

   _____

2. "You coward!" Jim scolded. "Are you really too **afraid** to call Stephanie and ask her to a movie?"

   _____

3. I can't believe Linda would be so **vindictive** as to hurt her tormentor.

   _____

4. The **insolent** student soon found out that Miss Johnston would allow no disrespectful behavior in her classroom.

   _____

5. The adult geese were always **vigilant** while their goslings were eating.

   _____

Vocabulary Power

Review: Unit 2

EXERCISE A

Circle the letter of the word that best completes each sentence.

1. When a person is suffering, he or she needs _____.
   a. vista   b. visage   c. solace   d. privation

2. You may not earn a living from writing, but you can enjoy writing as a(n) _____.
   a. epiphany   b. avocation   c. visitation   d. renaissance

3. Ken is too _____ to make a decision about the topic of his term paper.
   a. unscrupulous   b. disingenuous   c. fortuitous   d. irresolute

4. Asking for advice can be helpful, but _____ often is the best way to solve a personal problem.
   a. introspection   b. epiphany   c. renaissance   d. solace

5. Alyssa is so _____ that her friends never know how she is feeling.
   a. unsavory   b. impassive   c. disconsolate   d. visible

6. My grandmother's _____ is wrinkled, but she is a beautiful woman.
   a. vista   b. epiphany   c. vision   d. visage

7. Fiona is so _____ that she would never flaunt her family's wealth.
   a. unpretentious   b. unscrupulous   c. intractable   d. disconsolate

8. The _____ boy would not allow anyone to help him tie his shoes.
   a. bereft   b. disingenuous   c. intractable   d. unpretentious

9. It was _____ of Nancy to leave the house without checking to see that the stove was turned off.
   a. impassive   b. irresponsible   c. evident   d. melancholy

10. A person with allergies needs to be _____ enough to bring her medication.
   a. intractable   b. evident   c. bereft   d. provident

EXERCISE B

Circle the word that is the best synonym for the boldfaced word.

1. **melancholy:**   optimism   gloom   anger

2. **provisional:**   temporary   weak   fair

3. **visualize:**   describe   imagine   feel

4. **disingenuous:**   honest   ignorant   sneaky

5. **disconsolate:**   sad   confused   vengeful

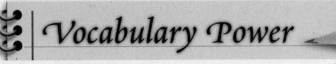

Vocabulary Power

Test: Unit 2

PART A

Circle the word in each set of parentheses that best completes the sentence.

1. Harry's (nonconformist, fortuitous, impassive) attitude led him to question things that most people take for granted.

2. Sela tried on at least fifty pairs of glasses before she found a pair that she thought was flattering to her (vista, introspection, visage).

3. We were not expecting a(n) (epiphany, privation, visitation) from the Rabbi that day, but there he was on the doorstep.

4. Laurence was (unpretentious, disconsolate, visible) and could not be cheered by any form of (privation, vision, solace).

5. A(n) (bereft, irresolute, fortuitous) event can unexpectedly open up a new (vista, avocation, introspection) of future possibilities.

6. Avoiding ice cream is hard enough, but giving up chocolate would truly be a (solace, privation, visage).

7. Does Veronica restore antique furniture for a living, or does she do it as a(n) (renaissance, avocation, epiphany)?

8. Greg worried that Alicia viewed their relationship as (provisional, disingenuous, irresponsible) and was just waiting to meet somebody better.

9. A firefighter cannot afford to be (unsavory, irresolute, evident); he or she must be able to make split-second decisions in an emergency.

10. Maura seems pleasant enough, but her brother is a rather (unpretentious, bereft, unsavory) character.

PART B

For each boldfaced word, circle the letter of the word that is most nearly *opposite* in meaning.

1. **nonconformist**
   a. leader   **b.** rebel   **c.** traditionalist   **d.** vocalist

2. **supervise**
   a. ignore   **b.** embrace   **c.** leave   **d.** support

3. **impassive**
   a. interesting   **b.** possible   **c.** honest   **d.** emotional

Vocabulary Power continued

4. provisional

   a. lucky   b. safe   c. permanent   d. shaky

5. unscrupulous

   a. confused   b. principled   c. kind   d. flexible

PART C

Circle the letter of the best answer to each question.

1. If an impassive classmate had just gotten an A on his English exam, what would you expect him to do?

   a. run around the room waving his paper triumphantly

   b. put the exam in his notebook without emotion

   c. smile with satisfaction but not discuss his grade with anyone

   d. wipe away a tear because he failed to get an A+

2. Which behavior might you expect from a nonconformist?

   a. checking his or her stock market investments

   b. following the most recent fads

   c. joining many clubs

   d. listening to music that no one else in school has heard of

3. What might you learn from introspection?

   a. what goals and values are most important to you

   b. the answers to next week's history test

   c. how to cooperate with other people

   d. the name of the boy who lives in the next block

4. What is an example of a fortuitous event?

   a. showing up on time for a date

   b. forgetting to take out the trash

   c. comforting a friend who is feeling sad

   d. running into an old friend who is in town for only one day

5. How would an intractable person react to a disagreement?

   a. by refusing to compromise or accept the other person's point of view

   b. by pretending to agree in order to avoid hard feelings

   c. by suggesting that a third person act as a mediator

   d. by changing positions in order to get along

Vocabulary Power

Lesson 9   Using Synonyms

Reflection on past experiences helps to shape your present life. For example, getting through a tough situation might have taught you a lesson that still helps you today. Emotions you've experienced might help you to understand the feelings other people have. You might have memories that occasionally make you feel confident, secure, angry, confused, or sad. The words in the following list relate to looking back at life events.

Word List

ambivalence	ephemeral	nostalgia	serene
bemused	incomprehensible	reminiscent	vibrant
blighted	lament		

EXERCISE A   Synonyms

Each boldfaced word is paired with a synonym whose meaning you probably know. Brainstorm other words related to the synonyms and write your ideas on the line provided. Then, look up the word in a dictionary and write its meaning.

1. **blighted** : spoiled _____
   Dictionary definition _____

2. **incomprehensible** : unintelligible _____
   Dictionary definition _____

3. **serene** : peaceful _____
   Dictionary definition _____

4. **bemused** : preoccupied _____
   Dictionary definition _____

5. **ephemeral** : short-lived _____
   Dictionary definition _____

6. **ambivalence** : indecision _____
   Dictionary definition _____

7. **lament** : mourn _____
   Dictionary definition _____

8. **nostalgia** : homesickness _____
   Dictionary definition _____

9. **vibrant** : lively _____
   Dictionary definition _____

10. **reminiscent** : suggestive _____
    Dictionary definition _____

Vocabulary Power *continued*

EXERCISE B   Economy of Language

Draw a line through the italicized phrase. Above it, write the vocabulary word that can replace the phrase.

1. Julie was full of *conflicted feelings of enthusiasm and fear* when she thought about moving to a new town.

2. Their visit was *frustrating and somewhat tarnished* by the knowledge that they may never see each other again.

3. I now find my decision to stop running with the track team *impossible to understand.*

4. After Jordan had finished his exams, he felt *calm and satisfied* for the first time in days.

5. The townspeople continue to *express sorrow over* the loss of several acres of forest to the fire.

EXERCISE C   Antonyms

Write the vocabulary word that is an antonym, or most nearly *opposite* in meaning.

1. permanent _____
2. straightforward _____
3. disturbing _____
4. unsentimental _____
5. improved _____

6. rejoice _____
7. certainty _____
8. alert _____
9. dull _____
10. meaningless _____

EXERCISE D   Clues Matching

Write the vocabulary word that best matches the clue.

1. This word can describe a dream at night or a passing thought.

   _____

2. This word describes a detective who can't stop thinking about an unsolved crime.

   _____

3. Music from another era can be called this.

   _____

4. This word may be used to describe a bright fireworks display that lights up a night sky.

   _____

5. Someone who wishes he could return to the 1970s has a feeling of this.

   _____

Vocabulary Power

Lesson 10   The Latin Root *mille*

Many words have *mille* as their root. The Latin root *mille* means "thousand." Since the root part of a word carries the word's main meaning, recognizing *mille* will help you to understand the meanings of these words.

Word List

mile	millennium	millimeter	millipede
milestone	milligram	millionaire	millisecond
millefleurs	milliliter		

EXERCISE A   Context Clues

Use your understanding of the root *mille* and context clues to determine the meanings of the boldfaced vocabulary words below. Write your definition of the word. Then, look up each word in a dictionary and write the definition.

1. The Declaration of Independence was signed in 1776, so in 2776 the United States will celebrate its first **millennium**.

   My definition _____

   Dictionary definition _____

2. They watched a **millipede**, a creature fringed by tiny moving limbs, move across the picnic table.

   My definition _____

   Dictionary definition _____

3. Tiffany asked, "How many thousands of dollars does a **millionaire** have?"

   My definition _____

   Dictionary definition _____

4. One of the handwoven rugs had a solid color with a single flower at its center, and the other had a bright **millefleurs** pattern.

   My definition _____

   Dictionary definition _____

5. Bob was so angry that he said he would not wait a second, a half-second, or even a **millisecond** longer.

   My definition _____

   Dictionary definition _____

6. Dr. Dixford started her new patient on a pill that contained only one **milligram** of medication.

   My definition _____

   Dictionary definition _____

Vocabulary Power *continued*

7. A **milliliter** of water is barely enough to dampen part of a tissue.

   My definition _____

   Dictionary definition _____

8. Did you know that the original **mile** was loosely based on a number of paces by foot?

   My definition _____

   Dictionary definition _____

9. The class tracked each **millimeter** of the tiny insect's movement across the desk.

   My definition _____

   Dictionary definition _____

10. Graduating from college was a **milestone** in Juanita's life.

    My definition _____

    Dictionary definition _____

EXERCISE B   Word Association

For each group of words, write the vocabulary word that belongs.

1. drop, teaspoon, fluid ounce _____

2. year, decade, century _____

3. ounce, gram, grain _____

4. striped, checkered, paisley _____

5. map, sign, landmark _____

6. long distance, highway, feet _____

7. wealth, bank, money _____

8. inch, line, dash _____

9. creature, spider, bug _____

10. moment, flash, instant _____

EXERCISE C   Analogies

Analogies show relationships between things or ideas. To complete an analogy, determine the relationship between the first two things or ideas. Then, choose the word from the word list that creates the same relationship in the second pair.

1. spines : porcupine :: legs : _____

2. ignorance : scholar :: poverty : _____

3. colors : rainbow :: flowers : _____

4. weight : ton :: distance : _____

5. one thousand : one :: meter : _____

EXERCISE D   Multiple-Meaning Words

As you learned in Exercise A, *millennium* and *milestone* are multiple-meaning words. Originally, *millennium* referred to a period of time and a *milestone* was a measurement of distance. Each word, however, has developed a more symbolic meaning. Symbolic meanings suggest something more than the exact meanings of the words. Refer to the definitions you located in the dictionary. Then, on a separate sheet of paper, explain the symbolic meaning of one of these words and its relationship to the original meaning. Give examples to illustrate each meaning.

Vocabulary Power

Lesson 11   The Suffix *-ous*

Suffixes have their own meanings and can be added to the ends of word roots to create new words with new meanings. The Latin suffix *-ous* is used to form adjectives that mean "having," "full of," or "identified by." For example, *-ous* added to the word *beauty* forms the word *beauteous*, which means "having beauty." The list below contains words that have the *-ous* suffix.

Word List

analogous	harmonious	suspicious	tenacious
audacious	illustrious	tempestuous	vigorous
capricious	malicious		

EXERCISE A   Synonyms

Each boldfaced word is paired with a synonym whose meaning you probably know. Brainstorm other words related to the synonym and write them on the line provided. Then, look up the vocabulary word in a dictionary, and write its meaning.

1. **tempestuous** : stormy _____

    Dictionary definition _____

2. **vigorous** : robust _____

    Dictionary definition _____

3. **capricious** : flighty _____

    Dictionary definition _____

4. **harmonious** : agreeable _____

    Dictionary definition _____

5. **illustrious** : famous _____

    Dictionary definition _____

6. **analogous** : alike _____

    Dictionary definition _____

7. **audacious** : bold _____

    Dictionary definition _____

8. **malicious** : mean-spirited _____

    Dictionary definition _____

Vocabulary Power continued

9. **suspicious** : questionable _____

   Dictionary definition _____

10. **tenacious** : persistent _____

   Dictionary definition _____

EXERCISE B   Word Meanings

Circle the letter of the word or phrase that best completes each sentence.

1. A **capricious** person is most likely to _____.

   a. always have a plan   c. be dependable

   b. change his or her mind   d. be stubborn

2. A **vigorous** jogger is _____.

   a. energetic   c. small in size

   b. slow   d. clumsy

3. Among the most **illustrious** are _____.

   a. hurricanes   c. children

   b. books   d. entertainers

4. A **harmonious** meeting might end with _____.

   a. a handshake   c. tears of grief

   b. a fight   d. an encore

5. One particularly **analogous** pair is the _____.

   a. cat and mouse   c. duck and pond

   b. coyote and wolf   d. flea and elephant

EXERCISE C   Multiple-Meaning Words

Several of the vocabulary words have more than one meaning. Using your understanding of these meanings, write the *-ous* adjective that best describes each of the following people or situations.

1. a turbulent relationship _____

2. a person who is untrusting of others _____

3. a strong, clear argument _____

4. a bright star _____

Vocabulary Power

Lesson 12   Using Reading Skills
Drawing Inferences

When you come across an unfamiliar word in your reading, examine the context for clues and details that imply certain information. Infer what the word means from these, then look up the word in a dictionary.

EXERCISE

For each sentence below, use context clues to infer the meaning of the boldfaced word. Write the meaning you inferred from the context. Then, look up the word in a dictionary and write its definition.

1. That garbage pile is one of the most **malodorous** things I've ever smelled; it ranks with my brother's sneakers.
   My definition _____
   Dictionary definition _____

2. A scientist can win no higher **accolade** than the Nobel Prize.
   My definition _____
   Dictionary definition _____

3. Francine's speech is full of **malapropisms,** such as when she suggested we take a different "tact" to solve the problem.
   My definition _____
   Dictionary definition _____

4. Some of the candidate's ideas were **dubious,** such as his suggestion that the government use social security funds to help pay off the national debt.
   My definition _____
   Dictionary definition _____

5. The date when Charlie spilled spaghetti sauce on his girlfriend's dress then wrecked his father's car was a **fiasco.**
   My definition _____
   Dictionary definition _____

6. When you drive across the United States, you'll find that certain things are **ubiquitous,** such as fast-food restaurants and shopping malls.
   My definition _____
   Dictionary definition _____

7. We need a name for our program that can become a meaningful **acronym,** such as Drug Abuse Resistance Education, or DARE.
   My definition _____
   Dictionary definition _____

8. Edgar Allan Poe is a master of **onomatopoeia;** for example, in his poem, "The Bells," he writes, "How they clang, and clash, and roar!"
   My definition _____
   Dictionary definition _____

Vocabulary Power

Review: Unit 3

EXERCISE A

For each boldfaced word, circle the letter of the word that is most nearly *opposite* in meaning.

1. **incomprehensible**
   a. understandable   b. confusing   c. calm   d. brief

2. **serene**
   a. disturbing   b. old   c. quiet   d. irritable

3. **ambivalence**
   a. energy   b. carelessness   c. certainty   d. conflict

4. **lament**
   a. lecture   b. sing   c. cry   d. rejoice

5. **millionaire**
   a. worker   b. pauper   c. volunteer   d. spendthrift

6. **vigorous**
   a. robust   b. weak   c. short   d. plentiful

7. **harmonious**
   a. friendly   b. tempestuous   c. forgettable   d. serene

8. **malicious**
   a. kindhearted   b. wise   c. apologetic   d. frightened

9. **suspicious**
   a. pleasant   b. violent   c. sympathetic   d. credulous

10. **tenacious**
    a. strong   b. feeble   c. mean   d. silent

EXERCISE B

For each of the words listed below, write a sentence on the back of this sheet in which it is used correctly.

bemused	reminiscent	milligram	analogous	illustrious
vibrant	millipede	millisecond	capricious	millefleurs

Vocabulary Power

Test: Unit 3

PART A

Circle the word that best fits each sentence.

1. The Goldbergs' peaceful summer vacation was _____ when a series of violent storms struck.
   a. serene   **b.** suspicious   **c.** tenacious   **d.** blighted

2. The plan needed to be revised because it was _____ to many on the committee.
   a. tempestuous   **b.** incomprehensible   **c.** reminiscent   **d.** illustrious

3. The girls couldn't decide whether to go or stay home, and this _____ lasted throughout the day.
   a. ambivalence   **b.** nostalgia   **c.** lament   **d.** milestone

4. People often believe a new _____ will bring about great change to society.
   a. milligram   **b.** millennium   **c.** millefleurs   **d.** millipede

5. The _____ weather caused damage to homes, trees, and cars.
   a. ephemeral   **b.** credulous   **c.** illustrious   **d.** tempestuous

6. Pushing ahead of other customers at the grocery store was a(n) _____ move.
   a. tenacious   **b.** audacious   **c.** vibrant   **d.** ephemeral

7. Kara was filled with _____ as she remembered all the fun she'd had at summer camp.
   a. nostalgia   **b.** ambivalence   **c.** lament   **d.** milestone

8. She wore clothing in _____ colors to match her lively nature.
   a. ephemeral   **b.** vibrant   **c.** malicious   **d.** serene

9. In biology lab, Chad measured the length of the insect in _____.
   a. miles   **b.** milliliters   **c.** milligrams   **d.** millimeters

10. The _____ pattern comprised violets and a variety of wildflowers.
    a. millefleurs   **b.** millipede   **c.** millennium   **d.** serene

PART B

For each boldfaced word, circle the letter of the word that is most nearly *opposite* in meaning.

1. **blighted**
   a. improved   **b.** spoiled   **c.** quieted   **d.** twisted

2. **vibrant**
   a. shiny   **b.** dull   **c.** exciting   **d.** eager

3. **ephemeral**
   a. small   **b.** passing   **c.** permanent   **d.** uninteresting

Vocabulary Power *continued*

4. illustrious
   a. scattered   b. colorful   c. distracted   d. unknown

5. tempestuous
   a. stormy   b. polite   c. peaceful   d. organized

PART C

Choose the letter of the word that completes each analogy.

1. rainbow : colorful :: star : _____
   a. illustrious   b. blighted   c. bemused   d. vigorous

2. loud : noisy :: calm : _____
   a. ephemeral   b. vibrant   c. serene   d. reminiscent

3. cry : laugh :: rejoice : _____
   a. ambivalence   b. uncertainty   c. nostalgia   d. lament

4. hundred : century :: thousand : _____
   a. millenium   b. milligram   c. millisecond   d. millionaire

5. future : expectant :: past : _____
   a. capricious   b. reminiscent   c. vibrant   d. serene

PART D

Circle the letter of the word or phrase that best completes each sentence.

1. A bemused person might appear to be _____.
   a. angry   b. energetic   c. thoughtful   d. listless

2. An example of something ephemeral is a _____.
   a. daydream   b. novel   c. rock   d. statue

3. A serene person might be found _____.
   a. relaxing   b. pacing   c. fighting   d. searching

4. A small amount of liquid might be labeled one _____.
   a. milligram   b. millisecond   c. milliliter   d. millimeter

5. A plant showing vigorous growth is _____.
   a. dry   b. withered   c. moldy   d. healthy

Vocabulary Power

Lesson 13   Usage

What does the word *adversity* mean to you? People of all ages, in all parts of the world, and in all walks of life experience hardships that test their physical and emotional strength. The words in this lesson illustrate adversity in different ways.

Word List

afflicted	falter	mortality	turbulent
debilitate	fugitive	refugee	volatile
disparage	jeopardy		

EXERCISE A   Synonyms

Each boldfaced word below is paired with a synonym that has a meaning you probably know. Brainstorm other related words. Then, look up the vocabulary word in a dictionary and write its meaning.

1. **debilitate** : exhaust _____

   Dictionary definition _____

2. **turbulent** : violent _____

   Dictionary definition _____

3. **afflicted** : sick _____

   Dictionary definition _____

4. **refugee** : escapee _____

   Dictionary definition _____

5. **volatile** : explosive _____

   Dictionary definition _____

6. **jeopardy** : danger _____

   Dictionary definition _____

7. **mortality** : death _____

   Dictionary definition _____

8. **falter** : stumble _____

   Dictionary definition _____

9. **disparage** : belittle _____

   Dictionary definition _____

10. **fugitive** : runaway _____

    Dictionary definition _____

Vocabulary Power continued

EXERCISE B Usage

Draw a line through the italicized phrase. Above it, write the vocabulary word that can replace the phrase.

1. A storm hit unexpectedly, and the fishermen were forced to battle *rough and wildly crashing* waves.

2. A(n) *insecure and constantly changing* political situation made life difficult for many citizens.

3. Jake visited his neighbor, who was *stricken* with a serious illness.

4. We realized that we were in *great danger* of losing our home if the tornado touched down.

5. On news footage, we saw the *people forced to seek safety* traveling on foot to the neighboring country.

6. A moment of danger often forces people to confront their own *fact that life can come to an end.*

7. Classmates who *show disrespect to* others sometimes do not understand the hurt they are causing.

8. Her fear caused her to *move unsteadily* at first, but then she gathered her courage and reached the podium.

9. In the 1800s, many African Americans were forced to choose between life as an enslaved person or life as a *person on the run.*

10. The doctor explained that her illness was not serious, but that it could *tire and drain energy from* her for several months.

EXERCISE C Word Association

For each group of words, write the vocabulary word that belongs.

1. insult, criticize, reject _____

2. stumble, trip, hesitate _____

3. unsteady, explosive, changing _____

4. danger, risk, peril _____

EXERCISE D Word Clues

Write the vocabulary word that best matches the clue.

1. This word, which sometimes refers to substances that evaporate quickly, comes from the Latin word *volare,* meaning "to fly." _____

2. The Latin *mortailis,* meaning "death," added to the suffix *-ity,* meaning "state of," gives you the meaning of this word. _____

3. The Latin word *debilitare,* meaning "to weaken," forms this word. _____

4. *Turba* is a Latin word meaning "confusion," and forms the root of this word. _____

5. The Latin word *fugere* means "to flee" and forms the root of this word. _____

Vocabulary Power

Lesson 14   Using Context Clues

Adversity can make people stronger. Those forced to face hardships often find within themselves strengths and survival instincts they never knew they had. Overcoming adversity can give people a sense of their own power and a greater understanding of human nature. Words in the following list relate to the positive ways in which people deal with adversity.

Word List

console	gall	optimist	resilient
conviction	infallible	persevere	zealous
fortitude	mobilize		

EXERCISE A   Context Clues

Use context clues surrounding an unfamiliar word to help you to figure out its meaning. Write what you think each boldfaced word means. Then, look up the word in a dictionary and write its definition.

1. Some had the **conviction** that all people should be free, but this belief was not enough to end slavery for many years.

   My definition _____

   Dictionary definition _____

2. Richard had the **gall** to demand that the newspaper editor read his story immediately.

   My definition _____

   Dictionary definition _____

3. We tried to **console** the sobbing boy, but he would not be comforted.

   My definition _____

   Dictionary definition _____

4. Deborah begins each new semester with the same **zealous** attitude—to learn and improve all she can.

   My definition _____

   Dictionary definition _____

5. After the accident, Sandy showed how **resilient** she was by going right back to driving her car.

   My definition _____

   Dictionary definition _____

6. Michele showed great **fortitude** in continuing to train for the race even after injuring her knee.

   My definition _____

   Dictionary definition _____

7. The rebel soldiers fought as hard as they could, but finally surrendered because the other army seemed to be **infallible**.

   My definition _____

   Dictionary definition _____

8. When they learned that the rivers were being polluted, environmentalists began to **mobilize** against the industries in the area.

   My definition _____

   Dictionary definition _____

9. Jackie, the **optimist**, insisted our losing team could eventually win the championship title.

   My definition _____

   Dictionary definition _____

10. When a task becomes difficult and exhausting, some people give up while others **persevere**.

    My definition _____

    Dictionary definition _____

EXERCISE B Word Clues
Write the vocabulary word that best matches the clue.

1. This word describes a person who bounces back from a bad situation. _____

2. If someone is eager and passionate about pursuing something, you might describe him or her as being this way. _____

3. A person who is bold to the point of insolence is said to have this. _____

4. This word describes a person who plans a day at the beach even if dark clouds and weather reports promise rain. _____

5. People who face challenges even through adversity possess this. _____

6. A team that never loses might be given this label. _____

7. If Congress declares war, American troops must immediately do this. _____

8. If you have a friend who is grieving, you should help him or her in this way. _____

9. Your strong belief in an ideal can be called this. _____

10. If you refuse to give up, even when times are tough, then you are someone who is able to do this.

    _____

Vocabulary Power

Lesson 15   The Latin Root *crux*

The root *crux* means "cross." This Latin root refers to the upright beam and crossbar used by ancient Romans for executions. The cross also became the central religious symbol to Christians throughout the world. This root influences the meaning of a variety of words, including the vocabulary words in this lesson. Because a root carries the main meaning of a word, you can figure out how words with the root *crux* are related to one another.

Word List			
crucial	cruciform	cruiser	crux
crucifix	crucify	crusade	excruciating
crucifixion	cruise		

EXERCISE A   Context Clues

Use your understanding of the root *crux* and context clues to determine the meanings of the boldfaced vocabulary words below. Write your definition. Then, look up each word in a dictionary and write its definition.

1. The situation is complicated, but the **crux** of the problem is that they are understaffed.

   My definition _____

   Dictionary definition _____

2. Lindsey's older brother had to make a **crucial** decision about where to attend college in the fall.

   My definition _____

   Dictionary definition _____

3. **Crucifixion** was an extremely painful form of torture, leading to death by suffocation.

   My definition _____

   Dictionary definition _____

4. If the reporters find out that Governor Smith lied, they will **crucify** him in the press.

   My definition _____

   Dictionary definition _____

5. Grandma, a devout Christian, always wore a **crucifix** around her neck.

   My definition _____

   Dictionary definition _____

6. We will **crusade** against any cuts being made to our school's budget.

   My definition _____

   Dictionary definition _____

Vocabulary Power *continued*

7. The red carnations on the grave were arranged in a **cruciform** pattern.

   My definition _____

   Dictionary definition _____

8. Joel will **cruise** around the neighborhood until he finds his cat.

   My definition _____

   Dictionary definition _____

9. Marcus was in **excruciating** pain as he sat in the emergency room with a dislocated shoulder.

   My definition _____

   Dictionary definition _____

10. We saw the police officer's **cruiser** circle the parking lot.

    My definition _____

    Dictionary definition _____

EXERCISE B   Word Association

For each group of words, write the vocabulary word that belongs.

1. torment, prosecute, torture   _____

2. critical, important, decisive   _____

3. fight, battle, action   _____

4. agonizing, painful, intense   _____

5. ride, search, move   _____

6. dilemma, difficult problem, core   _____

7. religious, symbol, cross   _____

8. square, heart, diamond   _____

9. taxi, police car, boat   _____

10. torture, punishment, execution   _____

EXERCISE C   Usage

If the boldfaced word is used correctly in the sentence, write *correct* above it. If not, draw a line through it and write the correct vocabulary word above it.

1. Christina felt that if she made a mistake while giving her speech, her audience might **cruciform** her.

2. Animal rights activists are determined to **cruise** against wearing animal fur.

3. **Crucial** decisions have to be made at the town meeting tonight.

4. We found a gold **crusade** on the lawn of the city cathedral.

5. Watching workers dismantle such a beautiful statue was **excruciating** for many people.

Vocabulary Power

Review: Unit 4

EXERCISE

Circle the letter of the word that is most nearly the *opposite* in meaning.

1. turbulent
   a. calm   b. slow   c. small   d. complicated

2. afflicted
   a. interested   b. determined   c. angry   d. healthy

3. jeopardy
   a. trouble   b. safety   c. anger   d. boredom

4. mortality
   a. life   b. pleasure   c. excitement   d. courage

5. fortitude
   a. intelligence b. strength   c. cowardice   d. serenity

6. console
   a. disturb   b. assist   c. plan   d. fight

7. optimist
   a. speaker   b. helper   c. fighter   d. doubter

8. persevere
   a. quit   b. destroy   c. comfort   d. console

9. crucial
   a. terrifying   b. insignificant c. peaceful   d. serene

10. excruciating
   a. humorous   b. powerful   c. boring   d. pleasing

Vocabulary Power

Test: Unit 4

PART A

Circle the letter of the word that best fits the sentence.

1. Finding shelter became a more _____ task when they realized the rain would begin soon.
   a. zealous   b. crucial   c. excruciating   d. resilient

2. I will vote for him because he seems to have a strong _____ about the importance of education.
   a. conviction   b. cruciform   c. crux   d. mortality

3. Winds were so _____ they tore shingles from the roof of our home.
   a. excruciating   b. afflicted   c. infallible   d. turbulent

4. Townspeople waged a full _____ against the building of another supermarket in town.
   a. conviction   b. crux   c. cruise   d. crusade

5. Because she was the _____ among the salespeople, she believed the store would not have to close.
   a. fugitive   b. refugee   c. cruiser   d. optimist

6. Dale wanted to swim, but stepping into the cold ocean water was _____.
   a. excruciating   b. resilient   c. volatile   d. turbulent

7. That form of the flu can _____ a person for several weeks.
   a. disparage   b. console   c. debilitate   d. mobilize

8. This country has been able to _____ through a variety of difficult periods in history.
   a. disparage   b. persevere   c. console   d. falter

9. Criminals were required to carry their own crosses for a _____.
   a. fugitive   b. crucifixion   c. conviction   d. refugee

10. As he walked off the stage, his nervousness caused him to _____ slightly.
    a. persevere   b. mobilize   c. disparage   d. falter

PART B

Circle the letter of the word or phrase that best completes each sentence.

1. A cruiser is often used to _____.
   a. burn chemicals   c. pray
   b. search for suspects   d. mock people

2. A person would be most likely to think about mortality _____.
   a. at a funeral   c. while giving a speech
   b. in a supermarket   d. at a town meeting

Vocabulary Power

Vocabulary Power *continued*

3. Someone who is afflicted _____.

   a. is always the envy of others

   b. encourages others

   c. needs medical care

   d. is never able to make a decision

4. A crucial matter is likely to _____.

   a. create stress

   b. seem unimportant

   c. be humorous

   d. be religious

5. To disparage people is to _____.

   a. give them comfort at a difficult time

   b. fight for their rights

   c. put them down

   d. encourage them to see your point of view

6. You would be most likely to find a crucifix _____.

   a. at a church

   b. in a science lab

   c. on a battlefield

   d. in a parking lot

7. When you cruise, you _____.

   a. hesitate and stumble

   b. give comfort

   c. tour an area slowly

   d. battle fiercely

8. A fugitive is someone _____.

   a. living life on the run

   b. helping people to be cheerful

   c. leading a public protest

   d. suffering from illness

9. A volatile person is _____.

   a. ill

   b. dull

   c. unpredictable

   d. never sad

10. A person with gall would _____.

    a. hide in the back of a room at a party

    b. pry into another person's personal business

    c. regret making someone feel uncomfortable

    d. keep from sharing his or her real feelings about a topic

Vocabulary Power

Lesson 16   Using Synonyms

In painting a portrait or creating a portrait with words, artists and writers try to capture more than the physical details of a subject. Meaningful portraits breathe with the spirit and personality of a subject, whether it is an individual, a group of people, a place, or a situation. Words in this lesson relate to impressions of people, groups, and places that might inspire a portrait.

Word List

controversy	imposing	profound	stoicism
diverse	potent	prophetic	vulnerable
gregarious	prestigious		

EXERCISE A   Synonyms

Each boldfaced word is paired with a synonym whose meaning you probably know. **Brainstorm other related words and write them on the line provided. Then, look up the vocabulary word in a dictionary and write its meaning.**

1. **diverse** : different _____
   Dictionary definition _____

2. **prestigious** : dignified _____
   Dictionary definition _____

3. **imposing** : impressive _____
   Dictionary definition _____

4. **potent** : powerful _____
   Dictionary definition _____

5. **stoicism** : reserve _____
   Dictionary definition _____

6. **vulnerable** : sensitive _____
   Dictionary definition _____

7. **gregarious** : sociable _____
   Dictionary definition _____

8. **prophetic** : predicting _____
   Dictionary definition _____

9. **controversy** : debate _____
   Dictionary definition _____

Vocabulary Power *continued*

10. **profound** : wise _____

  Dictionary definition _____

EXERCISE B Usage

Draw a line through the italicized word or phrase. Above it, write the vocabulary word that can replace the word or phrase.

1. The professor seemed *as if he could see the future* as he explained how life might be different two hundred years from now.

2. That poetry award is one of the most *well-known and respected* among writers.

3. The *powerful* remedy helped Matt feel better by the next day.

4. I worried about my brother, who seemed so *easily hurt and open to attack,* when he decided to run for mayor.

5. Most people agreed that the *grand and massive* new building seemed out of place in their small town.

6. When walking into a room of strangers, it is helpful to have a *friendly and cheerful* personality.

7. As Courtney listened to the debate, she realized how *extremely intelligent and deep* the candidate's arguments were.

8. The man's face, usually marked by *little emotion,* broke into a wide smile in the crowd of friendly people.

9. The *public disagreement* among the townspeople was over whether to fine those who do not recycle bottles and cans.

10. The group of city officials was *made up of many different kinds of people,* so citizens could trust that different points of view were being represented.

EXERCISE C Clues Matching

Write the vocabulary word that best matches the clue.

1. This describes a situation in which people with different opinions clash over an issue.

  _____

2. A person who always makes friends easily might be described this way.

  _____

3. You can use this word to describe the different tastes and smells at the International Food Fair.

  _____

4. People might use this word to describe a large mountain that seems to cast a shadow over everything below it.

  _____

Vocabulary Power

Lesson 17   The Prefix ex-

A prefix is a syllable attached before a root to alter or enhance its meaning. Many words that you see every day use the prefix *ex-,* which has a variety of related meanings. For example, *ex-* can mean "from," "beyond," "away from," or "without." The list below contains words that have the *ex-* prefix. As you look at the words try to figure out how *ex-* affects the meaning of each word.

Word List			
exorbitant	expediency	extricate	exuberance
expanse	extract	extrovert	exult
expatriate	extraneous		

EXERCISE A   Context Clues

Use your understanding of the prefix *ex-* and context clues to determine the meanings of the boldfaced vocabulary words below. Write your definitions. Then, look up each word in a dictionary and write its definition.

1. Laura has the personality of an **extrovert**; she always enjoys meeting new and interesting people.

   My definition _____

   Dictionary definition _____

2. It took officers many hours to **extract** important information from the suspect because he did not want to talk.

   My definition _____

   Dictionary definition _____

3. The upscale department store attracted wealthy people with **exorbitant** spending habits.

   My definition _____

   Dictionary definition _____

4. The children showed their **exuberance** by jumping up and down and clapping their hands as the parade traveled by.

   My definition _____

   Dictionary definition _____

5. A committee will have to study the **expediency** of building a new city hall building.

   My definition _____

   Dictionary definition _____

6. People immediately began to **exult** when they heard the soldiers were returning home from the war.

   My definition _____

   Dictionary definition _____

Vocabulary Power

Vocabulary Power *continued*

7. The farmer tried to **extricate** the lamb caught in a thick tangle of bushes.

My definition _____

Dictionary definition _____

8. We need to focus on the crucial facts and ignore any **extraneous** information in the report.

My definition _____

Dictionary definition _____

9. The writer used to be loyal to the United States, but certain political events caused him to become an **expatriate** in Europe.

My definition _____

Dictionary definition _____

10. We would lie on our backs in the open field and stare at the **expanse** of cloudless sky above us.

My definition _____

Dictionary definition _____

EXERCISE B Clues Matching

Write the vocabulary word that best matches the clue.

1. A detail that is not important might be called this.

_____

2. Someone who is happy and filled with emotion at an event might do this.

_____

3. You might do this to an object that is clogging your sink.

_____

4. This word describes a person who loves being around other people.

_____

5. A professional football field has a large one.

_____

6. Before beginning a new project, people might examine whether it has this quality.

_____

7. This word defines a person who has left his or her native land.

_____

8. A dentist might have to do this to a decayed tooth.

_____

Vocabulary Power

Lesson 18 The Greek Roots *hydr, hydro*

The Greek root *hydor* means "water." Most words that contain *hydr* and *hydro* relate in some way to water. The words in this lesson contain these two forms of the Greek root *hydor.*

Word List

hydrant	hydrogen	hydroplane	hydrotherapy
hydrate	hydrography	hydrosphere	hydrothermal
hydraulic	hydrophobia		

EXERCISE A Context Clues

Use both your understanding of the Greek root *hydor* and the context clues to determine the meanings of the boldfaced vocabulary words below. Write your definitions. Then, look up each word in a dictionary and write its definition.

1. Ty has a terrible case of **hydrophobia**; he's even afraid to put his toe in a tub of water.

   My definition _____

   Dictionary definition _____

2. There was not enough water pressure to operate the **hydraulic** equipment.

   My definition _____

   Dictionary definition _____

3. The dermatologist said that I should **hydrate** my skin with moisturizing lotion every night.

   My definition _____

   Dictionary definition _____

4. In chemistry class we learned that the combustion of the element **hydrogen** creates water.

   My definition _____

   Dictionary definition _____

5. I would like to study **hydrography** so that I can help ships navigate bodies of water.

   My definition _____

   Dictionary definition _____

6. Oceans, lakes, glaciers, water vapor, and clouds are part of Earth's **hydrosphere**.

   My definition _____

   Dictionary definition _____

7. We didn't do experiments with cold water; rather, we studied **hydrothermal** processes.

   My definition _____

   Dictionary definition _____

Vocabulary Power *continued*

8. During **hydrotherapy** for her injured leg, Janice would sit in a large metal tub of water.

My definition _____

Dictionary definition _____

9. In the flooded street, we saw the speeding car begin to **hydroplane**.

My definition _____

Dictionary definition _____

10. A heavy fine is levied if a driver blocks a fire **hydrant**.

My definition _____

Dictionary definition _____

EXERCISE B Clues Matching
Write the vocabulary word that best matches the clue.

1. To wet a dry sponge is to do this to it.

_____

2. This is a disorder that would prevent someone from enjoying a swim in a lake.

_____

3. In this process, water pressure causes a piece of equipment to be operable.

_____

4. This is anything involving hot water.

_____

5. A bubbling tub of water might be used in this type of treatment.

_____

6. All bodies of water are part of this.

_____

7. In this field, bodies of water are studied and mapped.

_____

8. Driving too fast over a wet road might cause you to do this.

_____

9. This supplies water to firefighters.

_____

10. This is an important element in one of the substances essential to life: water.

_____

Vocabulary Power

Lesson 19 Using Reading Skills
Word Parts

The word to which a prefix or suffix is added is called the base word. Some words look as if they were formed by adding a prefix or suffix to a base word, but in fact they are formed from a *root* plus a prefix or suffix. A root is a word part often derived from a language other than English, such as Greek or Latin. A root has meaning, but it cannot stand alone as a word in English. Here's an example of the difference between a root and a base word.

> *vulnerable = vulner* (Latin root meaning "wound") + *-able* (suffix meaning "to be able")
>
> *acceptable = accept* (base word) + *-able* (suffix meaning "to be able")

EXERCISE A

Complete the chart by deciding whether each word contains a base word or a root and filling in the columns accordingly. Use a dictionary as necessary. (Hint: The spelling of a base word may change slightly when a suffix is added.) An example has been completed for you.

Word	Prefix	Base Word	Root	Suffix
altercation		*altercate*		*-ion*
1. circuitous				
2. predetermined				
3. irreverent				
4. ambiguous				
5. commendable				

EXERCISE B

Each group of words below contains one word that is formed from a root rather than from a base word. Cross out the word that is not formed from a base word.

1. serious   prosperous   autonomous   famous

2. mobilize   reacquaint   melodious   rescind

3. shameless   alleviate   toothless   activate

4. compatible   impressionable   indoctrinate   indecisive

5. government   inflict   refinement   inconspicuous

Vocabulary Power

Review: Unit 5

EXERCISE

Circle the letter of the word that means most nearly the *opposite* of the vocabulary word.

1. exult
   a. grieve   b. sing   c. sleep   d. forget

2. prestigious
   a. small   b. respected   c. unimportant   d. dangerous

3. potent
   a. excited   b. frail   c. intelligent   d. old

4. profound
   a. quiet   b. enriched   c. funny   d. shallow

5. extricate
   a. color   b. involve   c. sort   d. investigate

6. hydrothermal
   a. powerful   b. colorful   c. icy   d. soft

7. expatriate
   a. politician   b. organizer   c. fighter   d. native

8. expediency
   a. comfort   b. inappropriateness   c. age   d. wisdom

9. hydrosphere
   a. car travel   b. science   c. land   d. ocean

10. prophetic
   a. generous   b. unknowing   c. brilliant   d. wise

Vocabulary Power

Test: Unit 5

PART A

Circle the letter of the word that best fits the sentence.

1. Members of the church will _____ on the coming of their religious leader.
   a. exult   **b.** extract   **c.** extricate   **d.** hydrate

2. An essential component of _____ equipment is fluids.
   a. potent   **b.** extraneous   **c.** hydraulic   **d.** hydrothermal

3. He worked his entire career to earn such a(n) _____ award.
   a. vulnerable   **b.** hydraulic   **c.** extraneous   **d.** prestigious

4. Runners were inspired by the crowd's loud _____ and ran as hard as they could.
   a. controversy   **b.** hydrography   **c.** exuberance   **d.** stoicism

5. Did the doctor need to _____ pieces of glass from the wound?
   a. extrovert   **b.** exult   **c.** extract   **d.** hydrate

PART B

Circle the letter of the word or phrase that best completes each of the following sentences.

1. A vulnerable person is _____.
   a. easily hurt   **c.** argumentative
   b. always the life of the party   **d.** unemotional

2. Someone who is an extrovert might _____.
   a. predict the future   **c.** spend too much time alone
   b. leave his or her native land   **d.** always search for social situations

3. A profound idea usually causes people to _____.
   a. laugh   **c.** cringe
   b. think   **d.** yell

4. A most exorbitant purchase would be _____.
   a. a book   **c.** a loaf of bread and peanut butter
   b. a dress   **d.** several diamond necklaces and a gold watch

5. A prophetic person is likely to _____.
   a. discuss your future   **c.** go to parties
   b. map lakes and oceans   **d.** be reserved

Vocabulary Power *continued*

6. A controversy involves _____.
   - **a.** social situations
   - **b.** debate
   - **c.** experimentation
   - **d.** water

7. To think about expediency is to think about what is _____.
   - **a.** warm
   - **b.** necessary
   - **c.** exciting
   - **d.** powerful

8. Something extraneous is _____.
   - **a.** unimportant
   - **b.** old
   - **c.** social
   - **d.** powerful

9. An expatriate no longer _____.
   - **a.** works
   - **b.** spends time alone
   - **c.** visits friends
   - **d.** lives in his or her native country

10. The hydrosphere includes _____.
    - **a.** a backyard pool
    - **b.** ships
    - **c.** trees near lakes
    - **d.** oceans

PART C

If the boldfaced word is correctly used in the sentence, write *correct* on the line. If not, write the correct word from the words listed below the sentence.

1. I think we're going to have to **expatriate** the trapped squirrel from the feeder. _____

   hydrate   extricate   exult

2. We were impressed by the **expanse** of the beautiful lake, which seemed to cover miles.

   _____

   expatriate   extract   exult

3. A study known as **hydrotherapy** is responsible for the detailed river map. _____

   hydrophobia   hydrography   hydrosphere

4. In the winter I always need to **hydrant** dry skin on my face and hands. _____

   hydroplane   hydrothermal   hydrate

5. He did not want to spend a(n) **prophetic** amount of time correcting errors. _____

   exorbitant   extraneous   expatriate

Vocabulary Power

Lesson 20   Using Context Clues

Life has many different kinds of lessons—large and small—in store for all of us. With every experience, life gives us a new piece of wisdom to explore and learn from. The words in this lesson relate to life lessons.

Word List

acquire	enterprise	optimistic	reflective
adversity	genuine	recognize	resourceful
creed	legacy		

EXERCISE A   Context Clues

For each sentence below, use context clues to determine the meaning of the boldfaced vocabulary word. Write your definition of the word. Then, look up the word in a dictionary and write its definition.

1. Danielle tends to have a negative approach to life; her sister Jackie, however, has an **optimistic** attitude.

   My definition _____

   Dictionary definition _____

2. One doesn't always **recognize** the importance of a life event until much later.

   My definition _____

   Dictionary definition _____

3. To **acquire** a school diploma, a student must first meet all requirements.

   My definition _____

   Dictionary definition _____

4. "Giving back to the community" has become a guiding **creed** for many people.

   My definition _____

   Dictionary definition _____

5. The committee undertook the **enterprise** cautiously; to start a neighborhood center was complicated, difficult, and risky.

   My definition _____

   Dictionary definition _____

6. Because José is a **reflective** person, he thinks fully about a problem before acting on it.

   My definition _____

   Dictionary definition _____

7. Jacob experienced a run of hard luck, but **adversity** taught him a great deal about himself.

   My definition _____

   Dictionary definition _____

Vocabulary Power continued

8. A **resourceful** person, Amy cared for her aging mother and kept her full-time job.

My definition _____

Dictionary definition _____

9. Will admires his parents; they share a deep and **genuine** love.

My definition _____

Dictionary definition _____

10. My grandmother left me a priceless **legacy** of life stories, which I hope to pass down to my own children.

My definition _____

Dictionary definition _____

EXERCISE B Word Association
For each group of words, write the vocabulary word that belongs.

1. remember, know, realize _____

2. belief, principle, opinion _____

3. project, endeavor, adventure _____

4. inheritance, gift, heritage _____

5. shrewd, inventive, energetic _____

6. thoughtful, careful, considerate _____

7. hardship, difficulty, misfortune _____

8. cheerful, bright, positive _____

9. honest, real, true _____

10. gain, obtain, earn _____

EXERCISE C Antonyms
Write the vocabulary word that is most nearly *opposite* in meaning.

1. false _____

2. pessimistic _____

3. lose _____

4. good fortune _____

5. thoughtless _____

Name _____ Date _____ Class _____

Vocabulary Power

Lesson 21 Using Synonyms

We learn lessons in a number of different places and at various times throughout our lives. School, home, and work are among the many environments in which we learn life lessons. The words in this lesson deal with life lessons.

Word List

advantageous	generous	optional	strategy
capacity	intuition	paramount	surpass
endeavor	notable		

EXERCISE A Synonyms

Each boldfaced word is paired with a synonym whose meaning you probably know. Brainstorm other related words. Then, look up the vocabulary word in a dictionary and write its meaning.

1. **endeavor** : attempt _____

   Dictionary definition _____

2. **intuition** : hunch _____

   Dictionary definition _____

3. **notable** : outstanding _____

   Dictionary definition _____

4. **advantageous** : helpful _____

   Dictionary definition _____

5. **optional** : not required _____

   Dictionary definition _____

6. **surpass** : exceed _____

   Dictionary definition _____

7. **capacity** : potential _____

   Dictionary definition _____

8. **paramount** : supreme _____

   Dictionary definition _____

9. **strategy** : plan _____

   Dictionary definition _____

10. **generous** : bountiful _____

    Dictionary definition _____

Vocabulary Power continued

EXERCISE B Clues Matching
Write the vocabulary word that best matches the clue.

1. An elective course could also be described in this way. _____

2. Describes someone who is famous in his or her field. _____

3. A group of students work to get different food choices in the cafeteria. _____

4. A starting hourly wage well above minimum might be described this way. _____

5. Describes a careful method for reaching a goal. _____

EXERCISE C Antonyms
Write the vocabulary word that is most nearly *opposite* in meaning.

1. fall short of _____   3. unfavorable _____

2. reason _____   4. unimportant _____

EXERCISE D Sentence Completion
Complete each sentence with the vocabulary word that fits.

1. To get a good summer job, it is _____ that I obtain excellent grades.

2. Unfortunately, the instructor's training _____ seemed outdated and uninspiring.

3. Erica's personal goal is to _____ her best time running the mile.

4. The company's policy of allowing four weeks of vacation for new employees seems _____.

5. Joel decided to _____ to pass the test to be a lifeguard next summer.

EXERCISE E Word Origins
Write the vocabulary word that best fits each sentence.

1. Knowing that the prefix *in-* can mean "in" and that the Latin word *tuéri* means "to look at" can help you understand the meaning of the word _____.

2. We get a hint of the meaning of the word _____ when we learn that the Latin word *mont* means "mountain."

3. The Middle English word *endeveren*, meaning "to exert oneself," became the Modern English word _____.

4. The French word *avant*, meaning "before," is related to the vocabulary word _____.

5. The vocabulary word _____ is related to the Latin expression *nota bene*, which means "mark well."

Vocabulary Power

Lesson 22   The Word Roots *viv, vit, vita*

The word root *viv* comes from the Latin verb *vivere*, which means "to live." Related to *vivere* are the roots *vit* and *vita*, which mean "life." The words in this lesson all pertain to life.

Word List

convivial	revived	vitalize	vivacious
revitalizing	survivor	vitamin	vividly
revival	vitality		

EXERCISE A   Context Clues

For each sentence below, use context clues to determine the meaning of the boldfaced word. Write your definition of the word. Then, look up the word in a dictionary and write its definition.

1. The film director wants to organize a **revival** of the old black-and-white films of the 1940s.

My definition _____

Dictionary definition _____

2. A **survivor** of the boating accident recounted his tale about the tragic experience.

My definition _____

Dictionary definition _____

3. The party began quietly, but after an hour of socializing everyone got into a **convivial** mood.

My definition _____

Dictionary definition _____

4. Each capsule contains 500 milligrams of the **vitamin** we all need most.

My definition _____

Dictionary definition _____

5. To **vitalize** her spirits, my neighbor starts each day with a brisk walk.

My definition _____

Dictionary definition _____

6. Only the most **vivacious** students were considered for the cheerleading squad.

My definition _____

Dictionary definition _____

7. The **vividly** colored painting included bright reds, yellows, and greens.

My definition _____

Dictionary definition _____

Vocabulary Power continued

8. Fortunately, the paramedics **revived** the bicyclist who had suddenly fainted.

My definition _____

Dictionary definition _____

9. The **vitality** of the young pup was evident in his quick, playful romp around the yard.

My definition _____

Dictionary definition _____

10. Our spring break was **revitalizing**; afterward we were ready for the new term.

My definition _____

Dictionary definition _____

EXERCISE B Synonyms

For each group of words, write the vocabulary word that fits.

1. sprightly, lively, spirited   _____

2. intensely, brightly, colorfully _____

3. animation, vigor, energy   _____

4. energize, rally, freshen   _____

5. merry, festive, friendly   _____

EXERCISE C Antonyms

Write the vocabulary word that is most nearly *opposite* in meaning.

1. dead   _____

2. unfriendly   _____

3. exhausting   _____

4. indistinctly _____

5. dispirited   _____

EXERCISE D Word Webs

Think about how the vocabulary words in this lesson relate to the idea of life and living. Choose one of the vocabulary words from the list. Then, on a separate sheet of paper, create a word web that includes any words, phrases, feelings, or ideas that you associate with the word you've written in the center of the web.

Vocabulary Power

Lesson 23   Using Reading Skills
Clarifying Meaning

What does it mean to "own" a word? To own a word is to be able to give its definition, use it in a sentence, or give examples from real life. These are all methods of clarifying the meaning of a word. Once a word becomes clear in your mind, it's yours for good.

EXERCISE

Each phrase below provides a general description of something. Give two or three specific examples of each general category. Make sure your examples show your understanding of the boldfaced vocabulary word. Use a dictionary as needed.

1. make **amends** _____
2. ancient **artifact** _____
3. show **hospitality** _____
4. **larder** contents _____
5. **defiant** gesture _____
6. tools of **edification** _____
7. **confidential** information _____
8. object of **forgery** _____
9. **fretful** gesture _____
10. place for **rendezvous** _____
11. **transparent** material _____
12. overused **cliché** _____
13. fancy **garb** _____
14. animal **habitat** _____
15. sign of **gratitude** _____

Vocabulary Power

Review: Unit 6

EXERCISE A

Circle the letter of the word that best completes each sentence.

1. Katrina is such a(n) _____ person that she brightens other people's lives.
   a. reflective   b. optional   c. vivacious   d. resourceful

2. The company's _____ goal is to increase its profits overseas.
   a. paramount   b. generous   c. optional   d. notable

3. After experiencing _____, Kevin learned how to offer support and understanding to others who are struggling.
   a. vitality   b. legacy   c. adversity   d. strategy

4. Formal dress was _____ for the spring dance.
   a. paramount   b. notable   c. reflective   d. optional

5. The elderly man lived a simple life, but left a large _____ to the urban garden project.
   a. legacy   b. strategy   c. reflective   d. creed

6. Kim's friends are certain that her _____ for singing and dancing will make her famous.
   a. creed   b. capacity   c. legacy   d. enterprise

7. We began the _____ with a sense of excitement and adventure.
   a. vitality   b. enterprise   c. adversity   d. vitamin

8. The neighbors often got together for a(n) _____ evening of good food and conversation.
   a. convivial   b. advantageous   c. genuine   d. notable

9. Joe's _____ to get a summer job begins with rewriting his resume.
   a. capacity   b. intuition   c. creed   d. strategy

10. The product was improved by adding calcium and an essential _____.
    a. survivor   b. capacity   c. vitamin   d. intuition

EXERCISE B

Circle the letter of the word that is most nearly *opposite* in meaning.

1. paramount
   a. first   b. unimportant   c. supreme   d. basic

2. optional
   a. elective   b. voluntary   c. notable   d. required

3. vividly
   a. dimly   b. brightly   c. happily   d. colorfully

Vocabulary Power

Test: Unit 6

PART A

Circle the letter of the word that best completes the sentence.

1. Because Ben was in a _____ mood, he carefully considered his true motives.
   - a. resourceful
   - b. genuine
   - c. notable
   - d. reflective

2. Her ambitious goal was to _____ last year's grade point average.
   - a. vitalize
   - b. recognize
   - c. surpass
   - d. revive

3. The family's _____ had always been "treat others as you wish to be treated."
   - a. enterprise
   - b. creed
   - c. strategy
   - d. intuition

4. After the marathon, the cold shower was a(n) _____ experience.
   - a. advantageous
   - b. resourceful
   - c. revitalizing
   - d. generous

5. The twins had opposite views on life: Matt's outlook was _____, while Mark's was pessimistic.
   - a. optimistic
   - b. convivial
   - c. paramount
   - d. optional

6. The guest speaker was a(n) _____ specialist in her field, having many publications to her name.
   - a. optimistic
   - b. notable
   - c. optional
   - d. vivacious

7. Jobs are once again plentiful and the economy is enjoying a(n) _____.
   - a. endeavor
   - b. adversity
   - c. strategy
   - d. revival

8. Tess trusted her _____ about the young man's character and gave him the job.
   - a. legacy
   - b. intuition
   - c. strategy
   - d. vitality

9. Being unafraid of animals proved _____ to Lynda's volunteer work at the humane society.
   - a. notable
   - b. reflective
   - c. advantageous
   - d. generous

10. The student was very _____, researching scholarships to pay his way through school.
    - a. resourceful
    - b. reflective
    - c. vivacious
    - d. generous

PART B

Circle the letter of the word that is closest in meaning to each vocabulary word.

1. **recognize**
   - a. obtain
   - b. achieve
   - c. know
   - d. forget

2. **genuine**
   - a. comfortable
   - b. shaded
   - c. false
   - d. sincere

3. **acquire**
   - a. remain
   - b. gain
   - c. forfeit
   - d. exchange

Vocabulary Power *continued*

4. endeavor

    a. connect   **b.** ran   **c.** give   **d.** attempt

5. adversity

    a. simplicity   **b.** difficulty   **c.** majority   **d.** vitality

6. paramount

    a. unimportant   **b.** satisfactory   **c.** first   **d.** moderate

7. intuition

    a. memory   **b.** guess   **c.** fact   **d.** knowledge

8. optional

    a. elective   **b.** required   **c.** essential   **d.** demanding

9. vividly

    a. darkly   **b.** dimly   **c.** brilliantly   **d.** cleverly

10. vitality

    a. exhaustion   **b.** emptiness   **c.** focus   **d.** energy

EXERCISE C

Circle the letter of the word that is most nearly *opposite* in meaning.

1. generous

    a. moderate   **b.** fortunate   **c.** giving   **d.** cheap

2. vitalize

    a. revive   **b.** energize   **c.** drain   **d.** avoid

3. vivacious

    a. gloomy   **b.** indifferent   **c.** friendly   **d.** cheerful

4. enterprise

    a. scheme   **b.** inaction   **c.** adventure   **d.** attempt

5. revived

    a. refreshed   **b.** delayed   **c.** lapsed   **d.** rallied

Vocabulary Power

Lesson 24   Usage

People express their emotions and ideas in many different ways. Perhaps you like to take pictures, write songs, perform plays, or write stories. Some of us communicate through humor. The vocabulary words in this lesson relate to different ways people express themselves.

Word List

articulate	emotion	lyrics	repertory
audition	encore	orator	tripod
comedian	farce		

EXERCISE A   Usage

Study the boldfaced words as they appear in the paragraph. Write what you think each word means on the lines provided. Then, look up the vocabulary word in a dictionary and write its meaning.

I was filled with **emotion** as I entered the room for my **audition**. Here I would hopefully demonstrate my outstanding acting skills and be chosen to be a member of the **repertory** theater group. They wanted a wide range of talents! I'd have to sing **lyrics** from popular songs, inspire laughter as a **comedian**, use my dancing ability in the physical gags of a **farce**, and project my voice well and far as an **orator** in serious drama. Through all these moods, I had to **articulate** my words clearly so that the audience could understand them. How would I ever do all this? I entered the room and placed my video camera on its **tripod** to record the audition. Taking a deep breath, I began. Believe it or not, they asked for an **encore**. I'd saved a favorite song and was delighted to perform one more piece, knowing that they liked me.

1. emotion _____

   Dictionary definition _____

2. audition _____

   Dictionary definition _____

3. repertory_____

   Dictionary definition _____

4. lyrics _____

   Dictionary definition _____

5. comedian _____

   Dictionary definition _____

6. farce _____

   Dictionary definition _____

7. orator _____

   Dictionary definition _____

Vocabulary Power *continued*

8. articulate _____

    Dictionary definition _____

9. tripod _____

    Dictionary definition _____

10. encore _____

    Dictionary definition _____

EXERCISE B Sentence Completion

Circle the letter of the word or phrase that best fits each sentence.

1. If you're asked for an encore, you're asked to _____.

    a. stop performing

    b. perform some more

    c. start the performance over

    d. bring the performance into the audience

2. Emotions reflect _____.

    a. how you feel

    b. where you live

    c. what you look like

    d. the foods you eat

3. In a repertory, you'd find _____.

    a. a one-woman show

    b. a single long-running show

    c. many actors performing many plays

    d. a run of dramas at a theater

4. If I articulate my words, you probably _____.

    a. can't understand me

    b. ask me to speak more loudly

    c. repeat them after me

    d. understand me clearly

5. Lyrics are _____.

    a. played by many instruments

    b. heard during science class

    c. developed by songwriters

    d. played by the trombone

6. A comedian enjoys _____.

    a. making people laugh

    b. teaching people to paint

    c. lecturing on physics

    d. driving people to work

7. A tripod is _____.

    a. a three-wheel bicycle

    b. a three-legged stool

    c. an animal with three heads

    d. a camera with three lenses

8. At an audition, _____.

    a. props and lighting are designed

    b. actors show their talents

    c. the theater is officially opened for the season

    d. the show closes early

Vocabulary Power

Lesson 25 Words Related to Writing

Writing takes many forms. Sometimes it is formal, such as research reports or nonfiction books. Sometimes it is informal, such as the personal note you write to a friend. No matter the form, writing is a process that takes you through several stages. The vocabulary words in this lesson all relate to writing—its process and its products.

Word List			
anecdote	editorial	monogram	revision
autobiography	illegible	postscript	scripture
bibliography	manuscript		

EXERCISE A Context Clues

Read each sentence and study the context of the boldfaced vocabulary word. Then answer the questions to check your understanding of the vocabulary words. Finally, write the dictionary definition of each word.

1. In her **autobiography,** Leslie told the hilarious but sometimes tragic story of her life.

   Who must the author of an autobiography write about? _____

   Dictionary definition _____

2. Both the priest and rabbi quoted **scripture** often to support their religious ideas.

   What is one place where scripture might be heard or found? _____

   Dictionary definition _____

3. The teacher returned my report ungraded because she said it was so **illegible** that she could not accurately evaluate it.

   What is one thing you could do to prevent a report from being illegible? _____

   Dictionary definition _____

4. The newspaper **editorial** expressed strong views about America's role in the crisis.

   What is one way you might respond to an editorial? _____

   Dictionary definition _____

5. Some museums exhibit the **manuscripts** of famous writers to show their creative works in the earliest stages.

   What is one way that a manuscript might look different from a published book?_____

   Dictionary definition _____

6. An **anecdote** is a bit like a snapshot in that it tells readers a brief story about the characters.

   How do you think a novelist could use an anecdote? _____

   Dictionary definition _____

Vocabulary Power *continued*

7. By studying the **revision** process, we can understand how a book changed from its earliest stages to its final published product.

    What is one thing you might do to a piece of writing during the revision process? _____

    Dictionary definition _____

8. After signing my name, I remembered another tidbit and dashed off a **postscript** to my letter.

    Where is the most likely place to find a letter's postscript? _____

    Dictionary definition _____

9. Mr. Hansen provided a specific format for the report's **bibliography** and asked us to provide page numbers in addition to each book's title, author, and publisher.

    What is one way readers could use a bibliography? _____

    Dictionary definition _____

10. I guessed that she must be Joanne Myra Caez because the **monogram** on her shirt read JMC.

    What does a monogram tell? _____

    Dictionary definition _____

EXERCISE B   Usage

If the boldfaced word is correctly used in the sentence, write *correct* above it. If not, draw a line through it and write the correct vocabulary word above it.

1. With its bright pink ink, Sheila's **monogram** stood out on every letter she wrote.

2. During the recent debate about the school budget, passionate **editorials** appeared in almost every issue of the local newspaper.

3. In writing his **scripture**, the actor recalled the many people who had shaped his career.

4. Danny's **postscript** reminded Nate to bring an extra bathing suit when he visits next month.

5. As the soldiers huddled in the dark, Jared kept the others awake by sharing **editorials** from his childhood.

6. Pharmacists often have to call the doctor's office for help in understanding the doctor's **illegible** handwriting on the prescription order.

7. My professor requires that I turn in my **anecdote** so that she can see how I changed the report from its first draft to the final version.

8. Many people find tremendous comfort and wisdom from reading **scripture**.

9. I discovered a fascinating book on undersea creatures in the **bibliography** of a *National Geographic Magazine* article on viper fish.

10. In today's world, a **manuscript** is not usually written by hand but is typed on a computer.

Vocabulary Power

Lesson 26   The Latin Roots *dic/dict* and *claim/clam*

Many word roots come from either Greek or Latin. These word parts carry the main part of a word's meaning but usually cannot stand on their own as a word. The roots *dic* and *dict* mean "speak" or "say." The roots *claim* or *clam* mean "cry out" or "shout." Words built around these roots relate to speaking or shouting. The vocabulary words in this lesson have either *dic/dict* or *claim/clam* as their roots.

Word List

acclaim	contradict	diction	proclamation
benediction	dedicate	predictable	verdict
clamor	dictator		

EXERCISE A   Synonyms

Each boldfaced vocabulary word is paired with a synonym or phrase whose meaning you probably know. Think about what the synonym means. Then, think about how the vocabulary word builds on the roots *dic/dict* or *claim/clam*. Describe a situation where you might use the vocabulary word. Then, look up the word in a dictionary and write its meaning.

1. **contradict** : disagree _____

   Dictionary definition _____

2. **verdict** : decision _____

   Dictionary definition _____

3. **proclamation** : announcement _____

   Dictionary definition _____

4. **clamor** : commotion _____

   Dictionary definition _____

5. **diction** : word choice _____

   Dictionary definition _____

6. **dedicate** : commit _____

   Dictionary definition _____

7. **benediction** : blessing _____

   Dictionary definition _____

8. **predictable** : expectable _____

   Dictionary definition _____

Vocabulary Power *continued*

9. **dictator** : tyrant _____

   Dictionary definition _____

10. **acclaim** : enthusiasm _____

    Dictionary definition _____

EXERCISE B   Word Equations

Use your knowledge of prefixes, suffixes, and word roots to complete the equations with the correct vocabulary word. Then, explain how each word builds on the roots *dic/dict* or *claim/clam*.

1. *contra-* "against" + *dict* = _____

   Explanation _____

2. *ver-* "truth" + *dict* = _____

   Explanation _____

3. *de-* "remove from" + *dic* + *ate* "act in a specified way" = _____

   Explanation _____

4. *clam* + *-or* "state or quality of" = _____

   Explanation _____

5. *pro-* "before" + *clam* + *-ation* "process or action" = _____

   Explanation _____

6. *ac-* "to" + *claim* = _____

   Explanation _____

7. *dict* + *-ion* "state or quality of" = _____

   Explanation _____

8. *bene-* "good" + *dic* + *-tion* "process or action" = _____

   Explanation _____

9. *dict* + *-ator* "one who" = _____

   Explanation _____

10. *pre-* "before" + *dict* + *-able* "capable of" = _____

    Explanation _____

EXERCISE C   Multiple-Meaning Words

Many words have more than one meaning. Look up the word *dedicate* in a dictionary. On a separate sheet of paper, write a sentence for each definition, using the word correctly.

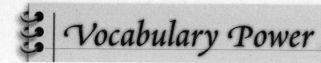

Vocabulary Power

Lesson 27   Using Reference Skills
Using a Dictionary: Multiple-Meaning Words

A multiple-meaning word is one that has more than one definition. When you look up a multiple-meaning word in a dictionary, you will see several definitions in the same entry. For example, note the multiple meanings of the word *affect* in this dictionary entry:

> **af • fect** ¹ (e-fect′) *tr. v.* **-fect • ed, -fect • ing, -fects.** **1.** To have an influence on or cause a change in. **2.** To act on the emotion of; touch or move. **3.** To attack or infect, as a disease. —*n.* (af′-fect′). **1.** *Psychol.* **a.** A feeling or emotion as distinguished from cognition, thought, or action. **b.** A strong feeling having active consequences. **2.** *Obsolete.* A disposition, feeling, or tendency.

EXERCISE

Read the sentences and look up each boldfaced word in a dictionary. Write the meaning that is being used in the sentence.

1. The **object** of this lesson is to teach you about multiple-meaning words.

   Dictionary definition _____

2. Do you **object** to smoking areas in restaurants?

   Dictionary definition _____

3. To turn on this computer, **depress** the button on the upper right corner of the keyboard.

   Dictionary definition _____

4. Don't read this article if you're in a bad mood; it will only **depress** you further.

   Dictionary definition _____

5. It took me a moment to **realize** that Ned was joking.

   Dictionary definition _____

6. I wonder if Marissa will ever **realize** her dream of becoming a doctor.

   Dictionary definition _____

7. Each day students are expected to check the **status** of their biology experiments and record any changes.

   Dictionary definition _____

8. Peter's broken-down jalopy is hardly a **status** symbol.

   Dictionary definition _____

9. Can two circles be **parallel,** or does the concept apply only to straight lines?

   Dictionary definition _____

10. The main character in this novel faces some situations that **parallel** my own life.

   Dictionary definition _____

Vocabulary Power

Review: Unit 7

EXERCISE

Circle the letter of the word that best completes each sentence.

1. The team entered the stadium to the _____ of an enthusiastic crowd.
   a. verdict   **b.** clamor   **c.** monogram   **d.** farce

2. To raise money for our new gymnasium, we have hired _____ Jed Binet to entertain us.
   a. comedian   **b.** tripod   **c.** repertory   **d.** manuscript

3. Use the _____ to stabilize the camera when the truck turns onto the gravel road.
   a. repertory   **b.** audition   **c.** orator   **d.** tripod

4. Henri watched the _____ on Camille's face as she finished reading his sad poem.
   a. acclaim   **b.** emotion   **c.** encore   **d.** diction

5. Ginny is in the habit of adding a rambling _____ that is often longer than the body of her letter.
   a. monogram   **b.** manuscript   **c.** autobiography   **d.** postscript

6. I am outraged by the president's behavior and will be writing a biting _____ for Monday's edition of the *Post*.
   a. editorial   **b.** bibliography   **c.** monogram   **d.** benediction

7. When the _____ was read on the news, we were shocked that the jury found the man innocent.
   a. proclamation   **b.** verdict   **c.** benediction   **d.** dictator

8. No matter what his true feelings are on an issue, my brother will _____ me just to debate.
   a. audition   **b.** contradict   **c.** articulate   **d.** acclaim

9. Robert is such a wonderful _____, we are sure he has a future in motivational speaking.
   a. orator   **b.** dictator   **c.** scripture   **d.** monogram

10. When Michael tried to leave the stage, the audience demanded a(n) _____ by applauding wildly.
   a. audition   **b.** benediction   **c.** encore   **d.** proclamation

Vocabulary Power

Test: Unit 7

PART A

Circle the letter of the word or phrase that best fits each sentence.

1. A verdict is most likely to be announced _____.

   a. in a courtroom   **c.** on a poster

   b. at the movies   **d.** by a salesman

2. A dictator is most likely to be _____.

   a. obeying commands   **c.** issuing orders

   b. voting on ideas   **d.** asking for advice

3. In a bibliography, you'll probably find _____.

   a. recipes   **c.** an author's life story

   b. the titles of books   **d.** the price of a book

4. You'd most likely find someone reading scripture _____.

   a. while driving a car   **c.** at the barbershop

   b. in a church or temple   **d.** on a boat

5. An autobiography _____.

   a. asks readers to take action   **c.** tells the author's life story

   b. appears at the end of a letter   **d.** displays a person's initials

6. When something is predictable, you probably _____.

   a. know about it in advance   **c.** hear about it after the fact

   b. watch it happen   **d.** participate in it

7. A manuscript _____.

   a. comes out of a bank   **c.** can be watched at a movie theater

   b. contains an author's first ideas   **d.** grows in a garden

8. A postscript _____.

   a. introduces a speaker   **c.** powers an automobile

   b. gives actors their lines   **d.** appears at the end of a letter

9. A monogram _____.

   a. shows someone's initials   **c.** weighs only one gram

   b. comes out of a computer   **d.** is caused by a virus

Vocabulary Power *continued*

10. Good diction would probably most concern a _____.

    a. baker
    c. firefighter

    b. scientist
    d. public speaker

PART B

Circle the letter of the word that is most nearly *opposite* in meaning.

1. articulate

    a. expressive
    b. distinct
    c. sensible
    d. mumbling

2. illegible

    a. clear
    b. scribbled
    c. crowded
    d. unclear

3. contradict

    a. deny
    b. counter
    c. endorse
    d. disagree

4. acclaim

    a. praise
    b. disapproval
    c. enthusiasm
    d. cheers

5. benediction

    a. dedication
    b. blessing
    c. praise
    d. curse

6. clamor

    a. silence
    b. noise
    c. commotion
    d. chaos

PART C

Circle the letter of the word that best matches the clue.

1. A letter from the publisher of a newspaper expressing his or her opinion

    a. verdict
    b. proclamation
    c. editorial
    d. encore

2. A skillful public speaker

    a. tripod
    b. orator
    c. clamor
    d. benediction

3. The words to a song

    a. postscript
    b. monogram
    c. scripture
    d. lyrics

4. A three-legged stool

    a. tripod
    b. dictator
    c. bibliography
    d. diction

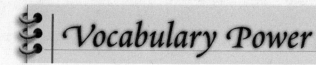

Vocabulary Power

Lesson 28   Using Synonyms

Think about something that inspires you. It might be the actions or words of great—or not-so-great—people. It could be a beautiful scene in nature, one that makes you feel a part of something larger than yourself. It might even be as simple as just doing something well, knowing that you've used your abilities to achieve a goal. The words in this lesson can help you describe what inspiration means to you.

> **Word List**
>
> | | | | |
> |---|---|---|---|
> | aesthetic | majestic | savor | undaunted |
> | affirmation | recede | serenity | vanquish |
> | elated | sage | | |

EXERCISE A   **Synonyms**

Each boldfaced word below is paired with a synonym whose meaning you probably know. Brainstorm other words related to the synonym and write your ideas on the line provided. Then, look up the word in a dictionary and write its meaning.

1. **majestic** : grand _____

   Dictionary definition _____

2. **elated** : overjoyed _____

   Dictionary definition _____

3. **vanquish** : defeat _____

   Dictionary definition _____

4. **affirmation** : approval _____

   Dictionary definition _____

5. **recede** : withdraw _____

   Dictionary definition _____

6. **aesthetic** : artistic _____

   Dictionary definition _____

7. **sage** : wise _____

   Dictionary definition _____

8. **serenity** : peacefulness _____

   Dictionary definition _____

9. **undaunted** : unafraid _____

   Dictionary definition _____

Vocabulary Power *continued*

10. **savor** : enjoy _____

     Dictionary definition _____

EXERCISE B Sentence Completion
Write the word that best completes each sentence.

1. Everyone in the river town breathed easier when the flood waters finally began to _____.

2. The noisy chain saw disturbed the _____ of the forest.

3. After all our hard work on the parade float, we were _____ when we won first prize.

4. Even though the cobra was quick and deadly, it was unable to _____ the nimble mongoose.

5. If you ate your muffin more slowly, you'd be able to _____ it.

6. The emperor indicated his _____ of the proposal by signing it.

7. The _____ statue towers over the island, welcoming visitors to Rio de Janeiro.

8. "Honesty is the best policy" is certainly _____ advice.

9. Moriah can spot _____ value in art objects that other people don't appreciate.

10. To everyone's surprise, the Blue Sox hitters were _____ by the speed of the opposing pitcher's fastball.

EXERCISE C Understanding Definitions
Read each sentence and answer the question that follows.

1. Because of his years of experience, Dr. Wilson always gives sage advice. How would you describe the

   doctor's advice? _____

2. As soon as she arrived at the isolated cabin after the drive from the city, Mandy experienced a powerful

   feeling of serenity. What words would you use to describe Mandy's life in the city?

   _____

3. The crowd roared its affirmation when the candidate asked for help in winning the White House. How did

   the crowd feel about the candidate?

   _____

4. Omar was elated when he saw the score on his math test. How do you think Omar did on the test?

   _____

5. When dawn broke, the soldiers saw that the enemy army had receded. What do you think the enemy army

   probably did?

   _____

Vocabulary Power

Lesson 29 The Suffix -ist

A suffix is a word or group of letters that can be added to the ending of a word or root. Suffixes have their own meanings and add to or change the meaning of a root word. The suffix -ist added to a word means "a doer or follower of something." The vocabulary words in this lesson deal with doers of certain actions or followers of certain ideals.

> **Word List**
>
> anarchist   paleontologist   propagandist   seismologist
>
> atheist   plagiarist   royalist   separatist
>
> cardiologist   pragmatist

EXERCISE A Usage

Write a phrase that best completes each sentence.

1. Propaganda is the spread of ideas meant to help one's cause or injure another cause. A propagandist is a person who _____.

2. Separation is the dividing of one entity, such as a nation or state, into two or more parts. A separatist is a person who _____.

3. Anarchy is the lack of law and order caused by the absence of government. An anarchist is someone who _____.

4. *Royalty* refers to the institution of government run by a king or queen. A royalist is a person who

   _____.

5. A theist is a person who believes in God. If you add the negative prefix, or beginning, *a-* to this word, you are describing someone who _____.

6. Pragmatic is an adjective that means "realistic." A pragmatist is someone who

   _____.

7. *Curdio* comes from the ancient Greek word for the heart. A cardiologist is a doctor whose specialty is

   _____.

8. Paleontology is the study of ancient life, such as dinosaurs. A paleontologist is a

   _____.

9. The study of earthquakes is known as seismology. A seismologist is a

   _____.

10. To plagiarize something is to copy it and claim it is your own work. A plagiarist is someone who

    _____.

Vocabulary Power

Name _____ Date _____ Class _____

Vocabulary Power *continued*

EXERCISE B Context Clues

Below you'll find the titles of five books. Fill in the space with the vocabulary word that best fits the title.

1. *My Incredible Life at the Court of King Bogdan III* by Ladislaw Warshevski, an enthusiastic _____.

2. *Raptors I Have Known* by Dr. Morton Franks, chief _____ at the Warren Institute for the Study of Prehistoric Life.

3. *How to Keep Your Heart Healthy* by Dr. Bruno Lopez, a leading _____ at New York Hospital.

4. *People Must Be Free: The End of Government* by George Mahler, world-famous _____ and revolutionary.

5. *Whole Lotta Shakin' Goin' On: The Violent World of Earthquakes* by Dr. Anna Wolf, head _____ at Pacific State University.

EXERCISE C Crossword Puzzle

In the space below or on a separate sheet of paper, create a crossword puzzle using *-ist* words from this lesson and from other sources. Exchange puzzles with a partner and complete the one you receive.

Copyright © by The McGraw-Hill Companies, Inc.

Vocabulary Power

Unit 8, Lesson 29 **73**

Vocabulary Power

Lesson 30   The Word Root *spir*

The Latin root *spir* means "breath." The vocabulary words in this lesson all have *spir* as their root. The root carries the word's main meaning. In most of these words, a prefix (at the beginning) or suffix (at the end) has been added to the word root to modify its meaning. The words are noun and verb forms of the same idea, based on the same Latin root.

Word List

aspirant	conspiracy	expiration	perspiration
aspiration	conspirator	expire	perspire
aspire	conspire		

EXERCISE A   **Sentence Construction**

Look up each vocabulary word in a dictionary and write a sentence correctly using the word.

1. conspire _____
2. conspiracy _____
3. conspirator _____
4. aspire _____
5. aspiration _____
6. aspirant _____
7. expire _____
8. expiration _____
9. perspire _____
10. perspiration _____

EXERCISE B   **Clues Matching**

Write the vocabulary word that best matches the clue.

1. All living things do this at the end of their lives.

_____

2. People planning a surprise birthday party have to do this.

_____

3. The human body produces this in order to cool itself.

_____

Vocabulary Power *continued*

4. Anyone involved in a secret plot is one.

_____

5. Your goal to become a writer is this.

_____

6. Each person who enters a contest is one.

_____

7. Certain foods become inedible after this date.

_____

8. You would notice yourself doing this when you play basketball but not when you swim.

_____

EXERCISE C Usage

If the boldfaced word is used correctly in the sentence, write *correct* above it. If not, draw a line through it and write the correct vocabulary word above it.

1. Rachel's greatest **expiration** is to become a chemist.

2. Our school's volleyball team was the leading **aspirant** for the conference championship.

3. **Aspiration** dripped off the steel worker's forehead as she labored near the blazing blast furnace.

4. The **conspiracy** was captured by the soldiers and led off in chains to the dungeon.

5. My dog Max pants all the time during hot weather because dogs can't **perspire.**

6. The suspicious dictator lived in constant fear that his closest advisors would **conspire** against him and remove him from power.

7. The milk looked like cottage cheese because the **expire** date was two months ago.

8. A group of **conspirators** assassinated the prince of Austria-Hungary and ignited the war.

9. "I **aspire** to hold the highest office in the state before I am thirty years old," announced the high school valedictorian to her awed classmates.

10. "My dear friends," gasped the fatally wounded hero, "allow me one favor before I **perspire.**"

Vocabulary Power

Lesson 31   Using Reading Skills
Context Clues

The ideas inherent in words surrounding an unfamiliar word make up that word's context. You can use the context to discover the meaning of an unknown vocabulary word. Look for key words elsewhere in the sentence that will help you define the unknown word.

EXERCISE

Read each sentence. Use context clues to find the meaning of the boldfaced word. On the first line, jot down key words in the sentence that help you define the unknown vocabulary word. Then, write the boldfaced word's probable meaning on the second line.

1. We assigned Miranda the job of checking every measurement in the project because she is **scrupulous** about details.

   _____

   My definition _____

2. The detective refused to **speculate** about how the robbery was committed until he could examine the crime scene.

   _____

   My definition _____

3. No matter how hard they struggled, the movers could not haul the **unwieldy** piano up the steep steps.

   _____

   My definition _____

4. The children's eyes lit up when their grandmother walked through the door **laden** with brightly wrapped packages.

   _____

   My definition _____

5. Trina sighed and left the beautiful campsite and majestic mountain scenery with extreme **reluctance**.

   _____

   My definition _____

6. The most generous contributor to the charity did not reveal her name, preferring to remain **anonymous**.

   _____

   My definition _____

Vocabulary Power

Vocabulary Power

Review: Unit 8

EXERCISE

Circle the letter of the word that can best replace the word or words in italics.

1. My grandmother was *overjoyed and excited* when I told her I had been accepted in the United States Air Force.
   a. scrupulous   b. elated   c. undaunted   d. stalwart

2. That huge sack of potatoes is the most *awkward and difficult* object to carry inside.
   a. insatiable   b. laden   c. unwieldy   d. majestic

3. The *specialist in prehistoric life* lectured on the size of a stegosaurus's brain.
   a. paleontologist   b. seismologist   c. cardiologist   d. propagandist

4. The revolutionaries called a secret meeting to organize their *plot* against the government.
   a. conspiracy   b. multitude   c. sage   d. wane

5. The head of the exploration team sent out a request for a dozen *strong and brave* men and women for the arctic expedition.
   a. majestic   b. aesthetic   c. stalwart   d. undaunted

6. The movie audience always weeps as the ship slowly sinks and the unfortunate passengers *breathe their last.*
   a. wane   b. aspire   c. recede   d. expire

7. On Christmas morning, Jane arrived, *loaded* with packages for the entire family.
   a. elated   b. laden   c. undaunted   d. majestic

8. With all the abstract ideas put forth by members, what we really need is a hard-nosed *realist.*
   a. anarchist   b. pragmatist   c. separatist   d. royalist

9. Even though Dr. Wang never achieved her highest *goal and hope,* a cure for cancer, she paved the way for important medical discoveries.
   a. multitude   b. reluctance   c. expiration   d. aspiration

10. Now, we can only *guess* about the deceased politician's potential in government.
    a. speculate   b. savor   c. aspire   d. vanquish

Vocabulary Power

Test: Unit 8

Circle the letter of the word that best fits each sentence.

1. The clever _____ carefully replaced the essay she had copied illegally.
   a. pragmatist   **b.** propagandist   **c.** plagiarist   **d.** anarchist

2. Her fears began to _____ as the grizzly bear moved off into the forest.
   a. speculate   **b.** recede   **c.** vanquish   **d.** savor

3. The returning prisoner of war was stunned at the _____ of people who had assembled at the airport to greet him.
   a. multitude   **b.** affirmation   **c.** conspiracy   **d.** perspiration

4. As the temperature rose in the stifling closet where she was hiding, the police officer began to _____.
   a. aspire   **b.** perspire   **c.** expire   **d.** recede

5. My advice to anyone who wins the state spelling bee is to _____ the moment and be proud of all your hard work.
   a. speculate   **b.** aspire   **c.** savor   **d.** vanquish

6. The _____ supporters lining the streets cheered loudly for the queen as she passed by.
   a. royalist   **b.** atheist   **c.** anarchist   **d.** separatist

7. Kaleb was awed as he looked out over the _____ Rocky Mountains.
   a. unwieldy   **b.** stalwart   **c.** majestic   **d.** insatiable

8. Senator Gibbons was a(n) _____ supporter of civil rights laws and worked tirelessly for their passage.
   a. majestic   **b.** stalwart   **c.** elated   **d.** unwieldy

9. The public's demand for new *Star Wars* movies seems to be absolutely _____.
   a. pragmatist   **b.** scrupulous   **c.** aesthetic   **d.** insatiable

10. It is important to check the _____ date on any medication you plan to take.
    a. aspiration   **b.** expiration   **c.** affirmation   **d.** perspiration

11. She quickly became known as a skilled _____ because of the pamphlets she wrote defending the ruling political party's policies.
    a. anarchist   **b.** propagandist   **c.** segregationist   **d.** seismologist

12. "Give me a hand with this _____ thing!" he cried as he stumbled with the heavy sofa.
    a. zealous   **b.** sage   **c.** unwieldy   **d.** stalwart

Vocabulary Power *continued*

13. "I am not opposed just to this government," asserted the _____ loudly at his trial. "I am opposed to all governments!"

    a. anarchist   **b.** royalist   **c.** atheist   **d.** paleontologist

14. I felt sorry for the cab driver since he was _____ with two people's luggage.

    a. elated   **b.** zealous   **c.** laden   **d.** scrupulous

15. Whenever David sees two people talking in the halls, he thinks they are getting together to _____ against him.

    a. expire   **b.** speculate   **c.** aspire   **d.** conspire

16. Merrilee had a tremendous feeling of _____ when her teammates elected her captain of the swimming team.

    a. aspiration   **b.** conspiracy   **c.** affirmation   **d.** reluctance

17. In spite of the forces opposing them, the Roman soldiers were _____ as they prepared for battle.

    a. sage   **b.** aesthetic   **c.** unwieldy   **d.** undaunted

18. We count on my great-grandmother to give us _____ advice because of her fascinating and varied experiences.

    a. sage   **b.** zealous   **c.** laden   **d.** insatiable

19. Even though she disagrees strongly with the viewpoint, our minister is always respectful to someone who claims to be a(n) _____.

    a. paleontologist   **b.** seismologist   **c.** atheist   **d.** cardiologist

20. "How can you hope to achieve anything great if you do not _____ to great things?" asked the speaker.

    a. aspire   **b.** savor   **c.** recede   **d.** vanquish

PART B

Circle the letter of the word that is a synonym for the vocabulary word.

1. **majestic**

    a. colorful   **b.** tiny   **c.** grand   **d.** bright

2. **vanquish**

    a. exclude   **b.** wane   **c.** inspire   **d.** conquer

3. **aesthetic**

    a. dirty   **b.** friendly   **c.** athletic   **d.** artistic

4. **reluctance**

    a. hesitation   **b.** certainty   **c.** dislike   **d.** fulfillment

5. **serenity**

    a. gratefulness   **b.** peacefulness   **c.** hopefulness   **d.** emptiness

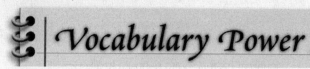

Vocabulary Power

Lesson 32   Using Synonyms

Love can have a huge influence on people's lives. It might be the love for a friend, a family member, a sweetheart, or an ideal. Love has the power to guide, inspire, and reassure us about who we are. The words in this lesson relate to the power of love.

Word List

adulation	dote	marital	reverence
affectionate	empathy	maternal	steadfast
amorous	idolize		

EXERCISE A   **Synonyms**

Each boldfaced vocabulary word is paired with a synonym whose meaning you probably know. Brainstorm other words related to the synonym and write your ideas on the line provided. Then, look up the vocabulary word in a dictionary and write its meaning.

1. **maternal** : motherly _____

   Dictionary definition _____

2. **empathy** : caring _____

   Dictionary definition _____

3. **reverence** : respect _____

   Dictionary definition _____

4. **idolize** : worship _____

   Dictionary definition _____

5. **affectionate** : tender _____

   Dictionary definition _____

6. **amorous** : loving _____

   Dictionary definition _____

7. **dote** : adore _____

   Dictionary definition _____

8. **adulation** : praise _____

   Dictionary definition _____

9. **marital** : wedded _____

   Dictionary definition _____

Vocabulary Power

Vocabulary Power *continued*

10. **steadfast** : unchanging _____

   Dictionary definition _____

EXERCISE B   Usage

If the boldfaced word is correctly used in the sentence, write *correct* above the word. If not, draw a line through it and write the correct vocabulary word above it.

1. Even though she had never run for office, Jan felt **reverence** for the losing candidate.

2. A wedding celebrates the **maternal** bond between a husband and wife.

3. The **affectionate** baby-sitter always gives each child a big hug when she arrives.

4. The owners **dote** on their prize-winning Persian cat; they never stop petting her!

5. The positive reviews of the new play were full of **adulation** for the leading actor.

6. *Romeo and Juliet* contains many **steadfast** scenes between the two young lovers.

7. Sitting under the ancient trees in the quiet forest, we felt a **reverence** for nature.

8. Marvin was **marital** in believing the man was innocent, although others had changed their minds.

9. The boys must **idolize** that baseball pitcher because they stood in line for three hours to get his autograph.

10. When the calf was born, the mother cow showed its **amorous** instinct by licking it clean.

Vocabulary Power

Lesson 33 Compound Words

Compound words are a combination of two or more words with separate and distinct meanings. *Snowstorm, pocket-size,* and *plus sign* are all compound words. Notice that a compound word may be spelled "closed up," with a hyphen, or with a space between the combined words.

Word List

clearinghouse	dovetail	off-putting	over-the-counter
cross-examine	halfway house	overblown	stopgap
double-talk	highbrow		

EXERCISE A **Definitions**

Analyze the words that form each compound word to match it with the correct definition.

_____ 1. describes a person who enjoys refined cultural activities, such as the opera and art museums

_____ 2. something that temporarily solves a problem

_____ 3. to question closely, especially to disprove the answers to previous questions

_____ 4. a central place from which information is distributed

_____ 5. describes a medicine sold lawfully in stores without a prescription

_____ 6. speech that has two meanings or is deliberately confusing

_____ 7. describes something that is disagreeable

_____ 8. a place where someone who has just left an institution, such as a prison or hospital, can begin to adjust to the outside world

_____ 9. inflated; out of proportion; exaggerated

_____ 10. to fit together neatly into a whole, like the fan-shaped fingers and openings in two pieces of joined wood

EXERCISE B **Clues Matching**

Write the vocabulary word that best matches the clue.

1. A lawyer in a courtroom might do this to a witness. _____

2. This could describe the effect of a rude remark. _____

3. A joke with a punch line about the symphony could be considered this. _____

4. Living temporarily in a tent until your house is repaired after a tornado is an example of this.

_____

Name _____ Date _____ Class _____

Vocabulary Power *continued*

EXERCISE C **Sentence Completion**
Complete each sentence with the vocabulary word that fits.

1. The schedules of the five doctors _____ just right, so that someone is always on duty.

2. The statement on the product label that says it kills fish but is harmless to humans sounds like _____ to me.

3. This ranch serves as a _____ for young men who have finished their sentences at the juvenile correctional institute.

4. When Samantha came home two hours late with a poor explanation, her parents decided to _____ her.

5. Luis didn't intend to offend people, but many people found his remarks _____.

6. Lev is hooked on comic books, but his sister prefers more _____ entertainment, like the ballet.

EXERCISE D **Drawing**
Find a definition of *dovetail* in a dictionary that includes a picture of a dovetail joint. Draw a picture of the joint below or on a separate sheet of paper. Add a caption explaining what the drawing shows and what the joint has to do with a dove's tail. If possible, find and examine a wooden drawer that is constructed using dovetail joints.

Vocabulary Power

Lesson 34   The Suffixes *-able* and *-ible*

A suffix is a word ending that can be added to a word or root. The suffixes *-able* and *-ible* mean "able" or "capable of." Adding a suffix to a base word or root modifies its meaning. For example, the word *supportable* (*support* + *able*) means "able to be supported." Words ending in *-able* and *-ible* are always adjectives.

Word List

amicable	credible	despicable	irascible
audible	defensible	fallible	pliable
commendable	deplorable		

EXERCISE A   **Base Words and Roots**

Use the information given about the base word or root and the meaning of the suffix to write the meaning of the vocabulary word.

1. The root *aud* means "hear." **Audible** means

_____

2. The root *fall* means "error." **Fallible** means

_____

3. The base word *commend* means "praise." **Commendable** means

_____

4. The base word *deplore* means "disapprove." **Deplorable** means

_____

5. The root *ira* means "anger." **Irascible** means

_____

6. The root *cred* means "believe." **Credible** means

_____

7. The root *ply* means "fold." **Pliable** means

_____

8. The base word *defend* means "protect." **Defensible** means

_____

9. The root *amica* means "friend." **Amicable** means

_____

10. The base word *despise* means "hate." **Despicable** means

_____

Vocabulary Power *continued*

EXERCISE B   Synonyms
Write the vocabulary word that has most nearly the same meaning as each word or phrase below.

1. believable _____

2. flexible _____

3. deserving praise _____

4. friendly _____

5. regrettable _____

6. likely to get angry _____

7. likely to be wrong _____

8. deserving scorn _____

EXERCISE C   Sentence Completion
Circle the word in parentheses that best completes the sentence.

1. The scientist had been wrong several times before, so many people suspected his theory was (defensible, fallible, credible).

2. The sound of the prop dropping on the stage was (audible, credible, commendable) only to the people in the front row.

3. In the cold weather, the garden hose froze and was no longer (pliable, amicable, audible).

4. Our (pliable, commendable, irascible) neighbor will yell at me if the leaves from our tree blow into his yard.

EXERCISE D   Descriptions
Write the vocabulary word that best describes each example.

1. The act of rescuing a baby from a burning house. _____

2. A witness at a trial who is known for being honest. _____

3. Someone who can be swayed by others. _____

4. The death of one thousand people in a bomb explosion. _____

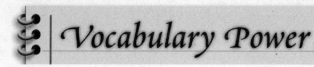

Vocabulary Power

Review: Unit 9

EXERCISE A

Circle the word in parentheses that best completes each sentence.

1. People might treat a respected religious leader with (empathy, reverence, clearinghouse).

2. Teenagers might (idolize, recede, dovetail) a popular singer.

3. If you knew how the loser of a contest felt, you might feel (adulation, empathy, irascible) for him or her.

4. Giving praise can also be called (empathy, adulation, double-talk).

5. Because we all make mistakes, we are all (amicable, fallible, amorous).

6. A (halfway house, clearinghouse, stopgap) is a good place for people to recover.

7. A medicine for which you don't need a prescription is called (over-the-counter, overblown, highbrow).

8. Animals have (maternal, marital, pliable) instincts that help them keep their offspring safe.

9. Mistreating or harming others is (deplorable, credible, amicable) behavior.

10. Donating money to charity is (despicable, commendable, audible).

EXERCISE B

Circle the letter of the word that fits the definition.

1. temporary measure to solve a problem
   - **a.** dovetail
   - **b.** maternal
   - **c.** stopgap
   - **d.** highbrow

2. having refined and sometimes pretentious cultural tastes
   - **a.** highbrow
   - **b.** overblown
   - **c.** steadfast
   - **d.** amicable

3. tending to get angry easily
   - **a.** credible
   - **b.** fallible
   - **c.** pliable
   - **d.** irascible

4. having to do with marriage
   - **a.** audible
   - **b.** marital
   - **c.** maternal
   - **d.** highbrow

5. confusing or contradictory speech
   - **a.** empathy
   - **b.** double-talk
   - **c.** reverence
   - **d.** adulation

Vocabulary Power

Test: Unit 9

PART A

Circle the letter of the word that is a synonym for the boldfaced word.

1. **exaggerated**
   a. highbrow   b. off-putting   c. overblown   d. idolized

2. **faithful**
   a. fallible   b. off-putting   c. marital   d. steadfast

3. **worship**
   a. idolize   b. dovetail   c. cross-examine   d. dote

4. **praise**
   a. empathy   b. adulation   c. double-talk   d. stopgap

5. **perceptible**
   a. deplorable   b. credible   c. audible   d. amicable

PART B

Circle the letter of the word that best fits each sentence.

1. The politician's speech was full of confusing _____; he wouldn't commit himself on the issues.
   a. reverence   b. double-talk   c. adulation   d. empathy

2. My aunt, who cared for me after my mother's death, has been the _____ influence in my life.
   a. credible   b. affectionate   c. pliable   d. maternal

3. Our interests _____ nicely because she likes to take photographs and I like to frame them.
   a. dote   b. dovetail   c. idolize   d. cross-examine

4. The newlyweds exchanged _____ glances as they strolled in the moonlight.
   a. amorous   b. pliable   c. marital   d. deplorable

5. This organization is a(n) _____ for information about physical and mental disabilities.
   a. stopgap   b. clearinghouse   c. empathy   d. halfway house

PART C

Circle the letter of the word or phrase that best completes each sentence.

1. If a new student is **amicable**, she is _____.
   a. funny
   b. friendly
   c. nice-looking
   d. foreign

Vocabulary Power continued

2. An example of a **highbrow** pastime is _____.

   a. watching cartoons

   b. jumping on a trampoline

   c. making rope jewelry

   d. attending the symphony

3. An **over-the-counter** drug is one that is_____.

   a. priced at a discount

   b. sold without a prescription

   c. unavailable in the Midwest

   d. issued by prescription only

4. To be **fallible** is _____.

   a. to fail school classes

   b. to be easily tricked

   c. to fall over easily

   d. to be prone to errors

5. An example of a **stopgap** is _____.

   a. taping clear plastic over a broken window

   b. standing in the road to halt traffic

   c. replacing a wooden door with a steel one

   d. joining two houses with a walkway

Vocabulary Power

Lesson 35   Using Synonyms

Each day unfolds as a mystery. What situations will you face? What positive or negative influences will affect your life? How will you react to those still unknown events or influences? What tools can you use to harness these situations? The vocabulary words in this lesson relate to the attitudes and tools we can use to respond to life's mysteries.

Word List

affliction	conventional	languor	ominous
aversion	coordination	novelty	trepidation
belligerent	impaired		

EXERCISE A   Synonyms

Each boldfaced vocabulary word is paired with a synonym whose meaning you probably know. Brainstorm other words related to the synonym and write your ideas on the line provided. Then, look up the vocabulary word in a dictionary and write its meaning.

1. **trepidation** : anxiety _____

   Dictionary definition _____

2. **impaired** : hindered _____

   Dictionary definition _____

3. **aversion** : loathing _____

   Dictionary definition _____

4. **ominous** : threatening _____

   Dictionary definition _____

5. **languor** : weariness _____

   Dictionary definition _____

6. **affliction** : hardship _____

   Dictionary definition _____

7. **belligerent** : hostile _____

   Dictionary definition _____

8. **conventional** : traditional _____

   Dictionary definition _____

9. **coordination** : cooperation _____

   Dictionary definition _____

10. **novelty** : unusualness _____

Dictionary definition _____

EXERCISE B   Matching
Write the vocabulary word that matches the clue or question.

1. If you hate clams, which word might describe your feelings about them?

_____

2. The newness of something can be called this.

_____

3. Which word might describe a physical or emotional burden you endure?

_____

4. If you dread taking exams, which word might describe your feelings the day before one?

_____

5. Which word might describe the dark clouds of a threatening thunderstorm?

_____

6. Which word describes the vision of someone who wears glasses?

_____

7. People who have traditional values might be described this way.

_____

8. Which word refers to the scheduling teachers and administrators sometimes do?

_____

9. The man in your neighborhood who's always getting into fights can be described as this.

_____

10. A cat who lounges lazily in the sun all day has this trait.

_____

EXERCISE C   Antonyms
Write the vocabulary word that is most nearly *opposite* in meaning.

1. attraction _____   3. improved _____

2. energy _____   4. encouraging _____

Vocabulary Power

Lesson 36   Using Context Clues

Emotions can be one of the greatest mysteries of life. Many outside influences affect our emotions or our state of mind. Different people react with various emotions to the same situation or event. The vocabulary words in this lesson relate to these mysterious emotions and to some factors that can influence them.

Word List

compassion	genial	malevolent	pressure
deplore	impassively	precocious	ruefully
detached	irate		

EXERCISE A   Context Clues

Use the context of each sentence below to determine the meaning of the boldfaced word. Write what you think that word means. Then, verify your thinking by looking up the word in a dictionary and writing its definition.

1. The community responded with **compassion**, offering support and loving concern to the victims of the tornado.

   My definition _____

   Dictionary definition _____

2. Candidate Saunders moved through the crowd, greeting everyone with the **genial** warmth and sincerity for which he is known.

   My definition _____

   Dictionary definition _____

3. Jenny sighed as she looked **ruefully** at the stack of dirty dishes and the pile of laundry.

   My definition _____

   Dictionary definition _____

4. Norton watched the proceedings **impassively** as the judge fined his company a full year's profits.

   My definition _____

   Dictionary definition _____

5. When salespeople phone our house, my father becomes **irate** and hangs up on them.

   My definition _____

   Dictionary definition _____

6. The club president disagreed passionately, saying, "I **deplore** the unfair effort to block his membership solely on the basis of age."

   My definition _____

   Dictionary definition _____

Vocabulary Power *continued*

7. The evil dictator carried out his **malevolent** plan against his own citizens.

My definition _____

Dictionary definition _____

8. The **precocious** teenager made a huge impression at the local art show with her stunning artwork.

My definition _____

Dictionary definition _____

9. How much longer can Sheila stand the **pressure** of working sixty hours a week at a job she can barely

tolerate?

My definition _____

Dictionary definition _____

10. During Uncle Robert's surgery last week, the doctor repaired his **detached** muscle by reconnecting it to the bone.

My definition _____

Dictionary definition _____

EXERCISE B   Word Association
For each group of words, write the vocabulary word that best fits.

1. happy, warm, pleasant   _____

2. angry, furious, wrathful   _____

3. separated, disconnected, isolated   _____

4. unexcitedly, stoically, apathetically   _____

5. spiteful, hateful, vicious   _____

6. compression, tension, urgency   _____

7. clever, bright, early-bird   _____

8. mercy, kindness, sympathy   _____

9. regretfully, sorrowfully, reproachfully _____

10. disapprove, regret, criticize   _____

EXERCISE C   Multiple-Meaning Words
Some words have more than one meaning. Each boldfaced word below is shown with two of its meanings. Circle the correct meaning to fit the context.

1. **pressure**: force; strain.   The company put pressure on the farmers to sell their land.

2. **deplore**: mourn; criticize.   The college which she endowed will deplore her loss.

3. **detached**: neutral; parted.   The panel of judges must stay detached as they evaluate each team.

Vocabulary Power

Lesson 37   Prefixes That Tell When

Prefixes are word parts attached to base words to change their meaning. Several prefixes relate to time. Knowing these prefixes will help you determine the meaning of unfamiliar words. The words in this lesson contain the prefixes *pre-* ("before"), *post-* ("after"), or *mid-* ("in the middle, during").

Word List

midseason	postdate	precaution	prehistoric
midsection	postmortem	preface	prelude
midyear	posttest		

EXERCISE A   Vocabulary Equations

Use the information above and the clues in parentheses to complete each vocabulary equation. Then, write a sentence using the vocabulary word. Double-check the meanings in a dictionary and write the definition.

1. *mid-* + *section* ("part" or "area") = _____

   Sentence _____

   Dictionary definition _____

2. *pre-* + *caution* ("care" or "warning") = _____

   Sentence _____

   Dictionary definition _____

3. *pre-* + *lude* ("play") = _____

   Sentence _____

   Dictionary definition _____

4. *post-* + *mortem* ("death") = _____

   Sentence _____

   Dictionary definition _____

5. *pre-* + *face* ("the printed side, especially in a book") = _____

   Sentence _____

   Dictionary definition _____

6. *post-* + *test* ("examination") = _____

   Sentence _____

   Dictionary definition _____

7. *mid-* + *year* ("period of 12 months") = _____

   Sentence _____

   Dictionary definition _____

Vocabulary Power continued

8. *mid-* + *season* ("time period linked to a particular feature") = _____

   Sentence _____

   Dictionary definition _____

9. *pre-* + *historic* ("related to history") = _____

   Sentence _____

   Dictionary definition _____

10. *post-* + *date* ("assign to a day or time in history") = _____

    Sentence _____

    Dictionary definition _____

EXERCISE B Prefix Matching

Circle the letter of the prefix that best fits each sentence.

1. July comes _____ year in the calendar.

   a. post-   **b.** pre-   **c.** mid-

2. The singing of the national anthem is part of the _____lude to every baseball game.

   a. mid-   **b.** post-   **c.** pre-

3. Autopsies are done _____mortem.

   a. pre-   **b.** mid-   **c.** post-

4. A part of a book appearing before the first chapter is the _____face.

   a. post-   **b.** pre-   **c.** mid-

EXERCISE C Headlines

Choose five events or experiences from the past year. Below or on a separate sheet of paper, write newspaper headlines using vocabulary words to tell readers when these events took place. Try also to identify the event in your headline.

Vocabulary Power

Lesson 38 Using Reading Skills
Connotation and Denotation

The literal meaning of a word is called its *denotation.* The *connotation* is what the word implies in a particular context. For example, the words *stubborn* and *firm* have a similar denotation, but each invites different feelings. *Stubborn* has a somewhat negative connotation, suggesting a lack of flexibility. *Firm* has a more positive connotation, suggesting leadership. Try to choose words whose connotations fit your purpose.

EXERCISE

Decide whether the boldfaced word has a positive or a negative connotation in the context. Explain.

1. My cousin treats his father in a **deferential** manner, seeking his approval on even the simplest decisions.

   _____

2. Mary has such an **effervescent** personality that everyone wants to spend time with her. _____

   _____

3. The month before exams was filled with **tumult** and anxiety. _____

   _____

4. His face had a **wily** expression as he proposed a new student council slate which, of course, included

   himself. _____

   _____

5. The police were able to **subdue** the crowd before trouble could occur. _____

   _____

6. Unfortunately, Stan has always been **squeamish** about snakes and frogs. _____

   _____

7. This morning I saw an incredibly **brazen** rabbit eating the plants under my kitchen window. _____

   _____

8. I skipped breakfast today because I think poached eggs are **repulsive.** _____

   _____

9. Lynn will not make a good school representative because she always looks so **unkempt.** _____

   _____

10. The state's education program is highly **adaptable** for students of many backgrounds and ability levels.

    _____

Vocabulary Power

Review: Unit 10

EXERCISE

Circle the word that best completes each sentence.

1. Hayley's performance at the track meet was (detached, impaired, malevolent) by his torn ligament.

2. Our family has (conventional, belligerent, ominous) values; we adhere to old-fashioned traditions.

3. We knew the (precocious, malevolent, genial) king would be imprisoned for his corrupt deeds.

4. Ellie (ruefully, impassively, tentatively) glared at the stack of paperwork that would keep her awake until morning.

5. We asked Claudia to (subdue, deplore, pressure) the excited dog before we brought in the new puppy.

6. The (precocious, ominous, conventional) warning of severe weather flashed across the television screen.

7. Jonas seems to have a(n) (affliction, aversion, compassion) to hard work; he disappears whenever there's a job to be done.

8. With great (novelty, trepidation, preface), Sarah appeared before the judge to answer for her speeding ticket.

9. Just as a (precaution, preface, languor) we carried extra supplies on our trip through the mountains.

10. The (novelty, languor, aversion) of the new toy quickly wore off and the children enjoyed playing with their old games.

11. Because of Jose's great (trepidation, compassion, aversion) for the homeless, he organizes the annual fundraising event for the shelter.

12. Kathleen can be (impaired, belligerent, unwieldy) when emphasizing a point.

13. Jim and Casey will return with the (midyear, midseason, postdate) report and predictions about the rest of the season.

14. Suzanne often looked (effervescent, unkempt, prehistoric) while her triplets were babies.

15. The (wily, brazen, repulsive) thieves faced the security cameras as they stole the cars.

Vocabulary Power

Test: Unit 10

PART A

Circle the letter of the word that is most similar in meaning.

1. compassion
   a. fear   b. anger   c. kindness   d. misery

2. impassively
   a. ruefully   b. reservedly   c. dramatically   d. emotionally

3. aversion
   a. hatred   b. enjoyment   c. sadness   d. excitement

4. coordination
   a. partnership   b. disorganization c. idleness   d. gentleness

5. deplore
   a. praise   b. convince   c. criticize   d. explain

6. detached
   a. connected   b. arranged   c. persuaded   d. separated

7. impaired
   a. improved   b. obstructed   c. imagined   d. imitated

8. genial
   a. grumpy   b. quick   c. mournful   d. warm

9. languor
   a. liveliness   b. stillness   c. beauty   d. meanness

10. affliction
   a. talent   b. torment   c. atmosphere   d. fondness

PART B

Circle the letter of the word or phrase that best completes each sentence.

1. People buy novelty items from _____.
   a. aliases   c. window shopping
   b. gift shops   d. beaches

2. If you are squeamish about eating oysters, you can be decribed as _____.
   a. easily sickened   c. brazen
   b. obsessed   d. adaptable

Vocabulary Power *continued*

3. One way parents can take precautions about the films their children view is to _____.

   a. read ratings and reviews   **c.** ask their children whether they liked the film

   b. pick up their children after the show   **d.** buy popcorn before the show begins

4. If you are expecting a posttest, you would _____.

   a. read ahead in the textbook   **c.** research new material at the library

   b. leave your books at a friend's house   **d.** review the material just completed

5. A belligerent attitude is one that _____.

   a. could lead to war   **c.** helps solves problems

   b. creates great art   **d.** entertains people for hours

PART C

Circle the letter of the word that best fits the clue.

1. You might feel this when called to the principal's office unexpectedly.

   a. compassion   **b.** trepidation   **c.** coordination   **d.** languor

2. You might feel this when greeting a respected adult or movie hero.

   a. deferential   **b.** detached   **c.** belligerent   **d.** irate

3. You might be called this if you learned to read at three years of age.

   a. detached   **b.** brazen   **c.** precocious   **d.** impaired

4. You could describe a clever escape artist this way.

   a. ominous   **b.** genial   **c.** squeamish   **d.** brazen

5. You would do this to a letter or check you want to send next week.

   a. posttest   **b.** preface   **c.** postdate   **d.** prelude

Vocabulary Power

Lesson 39   Using Context Clues

When we take journeys, physically or mentally, we often want to share them with others. There are many ways to share our journeys, from storytelling to novels, e-mail to phone calls, cartoon drawings to billboards, letters to faxes. No matter what the format is, writers and speakers need words that name places, describe movement, and trace journeys. The vocabulary words in this lesson relate to journeys.

Word List

commandeer	jostle	nationality	originate
disembark	landmark	nautical	quest
inertia	limousine		

EXERCISE A   **Context Clues**

Use context clues to determine the meaning of the boldfaced words in the paragraph. Choose one of the words to complete each sentence that follows. You may need to change the word's form.

Frieda began her **quest** by mapping out her route. Her boat trip would **originate** in her hometown. First, Frieda identified several **landmarks**, such as major cities, that would help her find the way. Then, she got a passport to prove her **nationality** as an American. In making a map, Frieda calculated the distances between ports in **nautical** miles across the water. Next, she built a cage to protect her pet parrot from being **jostled**. As she worked, Frieda dreamed of **disembarking** from the boat after completing the journey. A huge black **limousine** would be there to drive her home. Perhaps she would **commandeer** it for a comfortable land journey. The **inertia** of the trip would be hard to stop.

1. Jose drives a _____, taking movie stars and athletes around town in luxury.

2. The island of Nantucket sits about thirty _____ miles off the coast of Massachusetts.

3. I will never give up my _____ to find the rest of my family, missing since the war.

4. The Statue of Liberty, an important _____ in New York City, is visited by many tourists every day.

5. The escaped convict _____ our station wagon and left us stranded in the desert.

6. Addy's journey _____ in Iowa, and she completed the trip in Texas.

7. Because Boris is a citizen of Iceland, his _____ is Icelandic.

8. It took us a while to overcome our _____ and continue the journey.

9. Riding a motorcycle on a dirt road can _____ your insides until you feel sick.

10. The captain informed us that we would _____ from the boat through the rear exit.

Vocabulary Power continued

EXERCISE B Sentence Completion

Circle the letter of the word or phrase that best completes each sentence.

1. If the tour originates in Portugal, it _____.
   a. begins there
   b. ends there
   c. stops there for a week
   d. doesn't go there at all

2. A limousine is a _____.
   a. kind of bicycle
   b. large car driven by a paid driver
   c. fancy hotel room
   d. fast-moving train

3. If the poice commandeer your vehicle, they _____.
   a. monitor its movement
   b. put you in jail
   c. take your car for official use
   d. give you a ticket

4. You would probably be jostled _____.
   a. by sitting at a table
   b. when floating on a raft
   c. while talking on the phone
   d. on a crowded bus

5. During a quest, travelers hope to _____.
   a. find something they seek
   b. take a lot of photographs
   c. avoid friends and family
   d. spend very little money

6. A list of national landmarks should include _____.
   a. the Grand Canyon
   b. my bedroom
   c. the Moon
   d. the bookstore that just opened

EXERCISE C Clues Matching

Write the vocabulary word that best matches each clue.

1. Italian is one of these. _____

2. When you do this, your journey is usually over. _____

3. People use this kind of measurement to calculate their distance traveled over water. _____

4. This keeps a still bowling ball from moving. _____

EXERCISE D Journeys

Think about some journeys you have taken, whether mentally or physically. On a separate sheet of paper, write a few sentences telling about these journeys. Use the ten vocabulary words somewhere in your sentences.

Name _____ Date _____ Class _____

Vocabulary Power

Lesson 40 The Latin Roots *cede, ceed, cess*

Word roots communicate the main part of a word's meaning. The Latin roots *cede, ceed,* and *cess* mean "go" or "yield." Therefore, words built around these roots relate in some way to "going" or "yielding." When you look at unfamiliar words containing these roots, you can build meaning from your understanding of the roots. The vocabulary words in this lesson have *cede, ceed,* or *cess* as their roots.

Word List

access	exceed	process	secede
cease	excess	recess	succeed
concede	proceed		

EXERCISE A **Matching**

Study the sentences below and notice how the boldfaced word is used. Then, choose the best definition for that word from the list below. Write the letter of your chosen definition on the line. Use a dictionary as needed.

_____ 1. The rivalry between our two schools isn't likely to **cease** after one hundred years of competition.

_____ 2. During America's Civil War, several Southern states chose to **secede**, or withdraw, from the Union.

_____ 3. If you step to the counter, I will **process** your application for a part-time job.

_____ 4. The **excess** fabric can be used to make matching curtains.

_____ 5. After you have successfully completed ninth grade, you will **proceed** to tenth grade.

_____ 6. After three hours of grueling play, Josh decided to **concede** defeat to Andrew in the chess match.

_____ 7. Because of the unstable political situation, tourists have been denied **access** to the country.

_____ 8. A police officer may pull you over if you **exceed** the speed limit.

_____ 9. The new president will **succeed** the outgoing president.

_____ 10. How would you vote on a school board policy to exclude **recess** in the third-grade daily schedule?

a. ability to enter

b. stop, end

c. advance, move along

d. more than needed

e. withdraw from a group

f. yield, acknowledge hesitantly

g. to go beyond a set limit

h. review and complete

i. suspension of work for rest

j. to go after another

Copyright © by The McGraw-Hill Companies, Inc.

Vocabulary Power continued

EXERCISE B Antonyms

Circle the letter of the word that is most nearly _opposite_ in meaning to the vocabulary word.

1. proceed

   a. stop   **b.** continue   **c.** review

2. concede

   a. yield   **b.** change   **c.** resist

3. succeed

   a. follow   **b.** precede   **c.** accompany

4. secede

   a. quit   **b.** differ   **c.** join

5. cease

   a. stop   **b.** flounder   **c.** continue

EXERCISE C Multiple-Meaning Words

Words often have more than one meaning. Study the sentences. Then, circle the correct meaning from the choices given for each boldfaced word.

1. The talks will probably **succeed** (come after, achieve) in resolving the countries' differences.

2. The search party found the lost hikers in the deepest **recess** (hiding place, break from work for rest) of a cave.

3. We plan to **process** (develop, sue in court) the graduation pictures in Nan's lab after school today.

4. Only Mr. Rosensohn's students have **access** (increase by addition, freedom to make use of) to his books.

EXERCISE D Word Knowledge

Use your knowledge of the boldfaced words to answer each question. Explain your answer.

1. If you **succeed** at something, are you likely to be happy or sad? _____

2. When people **exceed** their diet's dessert allowance, have they eaten too much dessert or not enough?

   _____

3. When you **concede** victory to an opponent, do you accept or reject defeat? _____

4. When armies announce that they will **cease** fighting, are they going to stop or start fighting?

   _____

5. If you **access** your computer files, can you read them or are they closed? _____

6. If you watch someone **proceed**, is he or she moving or stopping? _____

Vocabulary Power

Lesson 41 The Prefixes *circu-, circum-,* and *trans-*

The prefixes *circu-, circum-,* and *trans-* suggest travel. Recall that prefixes are word parts affixed to the beginning of roots or base words to change their meanings. *Circum-* and *circu-* mean "around" and *trans-* means "across or beyond." When you encounter unfamiliar words beginning with these prefixes, use the prefix's meaning to determine what the whole word means.

Word List

circulate	circumvent	transcribe	transplant
circumference	transaction	transit	
circumstance	transcontinental	transmission	

EXERCISE A Synonyms

Each boldfaced word is paired with a synonym whose meaning you probably know. Write a sentence that illustrates the meaning of the word. Then, look up the word in a dictionary and write its meaning.

1. **transaction** : agreement _____

   Dictionary definition _____

2. **transit** : movement _____

   Dictionary definition _____

3. **transmission** : broadcast _____

   Dictionary definition _____

4. **transcontinental** : cross-country _____

   Dictionary definition _____

5. **transcribe** : record _____

   Dictionary definition _____

6. **transplant** : resettle _____

   Dictionary definition _____

7. **circumvent** : bypass _____

   Dictionary definition _____

8. **circulate** : flow _____

   Dictionary definition _____

9. **circumstance** : situation _____

   Dictionary definition _____

Vocabulary Power *continued*

10. **circumference** : perimeter _____

   Dictionary definition _____

EXERCISE B Clues Matching

Write the vocabulary word that matches each clue.

1. You do this to flowers to move them from a pot to your garden. _____

2. When you write down a speaker's exact words, you do this. _____

3. The purchase of a new bicycle is one. _____

4. When this railroad was completed, people celebrated. _____

5. The death of a much-loved pet could be an unfortunate one. _____

6. You can use a tape measure to calculate this for a basketball. _____

7. If your blood doesn't do this properly, you may become ill or even die. _____

8. Many cities have a public system for this. _____

EXERCISE C Sentence Completion

Write the vocabulary word that best completes each sentence.

1. They will determine the running track's exact _____ before placing the start and finish lines.

2. The radio station's _____ hours are only from 8 A.M. to 8 P.M. because of a shortage of funds.

3. Today, Americans can make _____ journeys on a fine system of interstate roads and highways.

4. Buying a home can be a complicated business _____.

5. Hearing-impaired students may be assigned a partner who will _____ class lectures.

6. Before the meeting begins, be sure to _____ among audience members before going to the podium.

7. I won't be able to call you at lunchtime; I will be in _____ from Chicago to Milwaukee.

8. Brenda has been active and healthy since her successful liver _____.

9. We can _____ his objections if two thirds of the members vote for the new law.

10. In this unexpected _____, we will need extra help to care for the homeless.

EXERCISE D Bon Voyage

Think about how each of the vocabulary words relates to journeys, to moving "around" or "across." Then, on a separate sheet of paper, create an illustrated greeting card wishing a friend "bon voyage," using at least two of the words from this lesson.

Vocabulary Power

Vocabulary Power

Lesson 42   Using Reference Skills
Using a Thesaurus: Antonyms
A thesaurus can help you learn more about what words mean, though in a different way from a dictionary. In a thesaurus, in addition to synonyms, you will often find antonyms for the entry word. Antonyms, which are words with opposite meanings, are useful for many speaking and writing tasks. For example, you might need an antonym when contrasting two topics or objects. This lesson gives you some practice in finding antonyms in a thesaurus.

Word List

abate	contemptible	indispensable	ornate
abstract	ebb	lavish	reproach
captivity	ecstasy		

Look at the sample thesaurus entry below.

> **ecstasy** *n.* joy, exaltation, rapture, delight, bliss, exhilaration, rejoicing, transport, ravishment, elation, jubilation, ebullience; **Antonyms:** gloom, misery, depression, sadness, despondency, sorrow, despair, woe

EXERCISE A

Use a thesaurus to list at least two antonyms for each of the vocabulary words.

1. ebb   _____

2. abstract   _____

3. captivity   _____

4. abate   _____

5. contemptible _____

6. indispensable _____

7. lavish   _____

8. ornate   _____

9. reproach   _____

10. ecstasy   _____

EXERCISE B

On a separate sheet of paper, write a sentence using each vocabulary word and one of its antonyms.

| Vocabulary Power

Review: Unit 11

EXERCISE

Circle the letter of the word that best completes each sentence.

1. If a police officer commandeers your car, she is probably _____.
   a. using it to catch a criminal
   b. giving you a ticket
   c. telling you how nice it looks
   d. having it towed

2. If you concede a point in a debate, you are _____.
   a. winning others to your side
   b. agreeing that your opponent is correct
   c. changing your opponent's mind
   d. ending the entire debate

3. If you try to circumvent a problem, you _____.
   a. forget it exists
   b. find a way around it
   c. don't let it bother you
   d. attack it head on

4. If you circulate a rumor at school, you are _____.
   a. actively trying to stop it
   b. helping the person the rumor is about
   c. confronting the source of the tale
   d. telling others the gossip

5. An ornate picture frame would be _____.
   a. simple
   b. plain
   c. complex
   d. broken

6. A nautical mile is a mile _____.
   a. at sea
   b. in space
   c. in the woods
   d. in Europe

7. A person's nationality describes his or her _____.
   a. weight at birth
   b. language of choice
   c. country of origin
   d. annual salary

8. If you proceed with your chores, you _____.
   a. negotiate to not do them
   b. continue to do them
   c. refuse to do them
   d. leave before you do them

9. To disembark means to _____.
   a. remove the covering from firewood
   b. quiet an angry dog
   c. exit from a boat
   d. cancel your subscription

10. If an item is in transit it is _____.
    a. moving from place to place
    b. decreasing in size
    c. improving in sound quality
    d. increasing in speed

Vocabulary Power

Test: Unit 11

PART A

Circle the letter of the word or phrase that best completes the sentence.

1. If someone or something jostles you, you feel _____.

    a. shaken   **b.** hungry   **c.** full   **d.** sad

2. When you cease an action, you have _____.

    a. begun it   **c.** learned it
    b. stopped it   **d.** invented it

3. Inertia is a property in which things _____.

    a. turn upside down   **c.** behave badly
    b. cheer loudly   **d.** remain in motion or at rest

4. The circumference of a _____ can be measured.

    a. building block   **c.** tennis ball
    b. pyramid   **d.** carpet

5. If you transcribe something, you _____.

    a. record it on tape   **c.** perform it for a live audience
    b. sell it to book lovers   **d.** record it in writing

6. When you exceed your goal, you have _____.

    a. gone beyond it   **c.** failed to reach it
    b. revised it   **d.** met it

7. During a recess, your work is _____.

    a. continuing   **c.** interrupted
    b. ongoing   **d.** completed

8. When you circumvent an obstacle, you _____.

    a. cannot proceed   **c.** go around it
    b. identify it   **d.** cannot find it

9. Someone who is in transit _____.

    a. is traveling   **c.** has arrived
    b. is about to depart   **d.** hasn't departed yet

10. If you're traveling in a limousine, you are probably _____.

    a. comfortable   **c.** crowded
    b. at sea   **d.** near the wing

Vocabulary Power continued

PART B

Circle the vocabulary word that best completes each sentence.

1. My (quest, process, transaction) for the latest book by Philip Pullman has taken me all over town.

2. Did North Carolina decide to (disembark, concede, secede) from the Union?

3. This ship was (jostled, accessed, commandeered) by the British Navy during the War of 1812.

4. The ball sailed over the fence, driven by its own (transit, inertia, ebb) that keeps it moving steadily unless acted on by an external force.

5. Despite our nervousness, the (transaction, transplant, abstract) at the bank went very smoothly.

6. Many of the finest tulip bulbs (originate, secede, circulate) in the growing fields of Holland.

7. Reluctant to sacrifice more soldiers, the general (succeeded, conceded, abated) defeat.

8. In Amarillo, Texas, one famous (landmark, quest, transaction) is the Cadillac Ranch.

9. The law requires that public buildings offer (reproach, excess, access) to people in wheelchairs.

10. When the storm winds had (ebbed, abated, proceeded) we set sail again.

Vocabulary Power

Lesson 43   Using Synonyms

Science fiction has many fans. People read books, watch movies, join clubs, and collect items focused on the human race's future existence and on the possible existence of other thinking beings elsewhere in space. The vocabulary words in this lesson relate to these other-worldly possibilities, to the ways we learn about them, to the moods they might create, and to the places we might find them.

Word List

abyss	emissary	lurk	telescope
conjecture	enigma	tantalize	vestibule
constellation	galaxy		

EXERCISE A   Synonyms

Read each sentence and think about what the boldfaced word might mean. Then, circle the letter of the synonym that best fits that boldfaced word.

1. We sent Captain Nelson to visit the alien's planet as an **emissary** for the human race.
   a. representative   b. victim   c. teacher   d. cook

2. As I stumbled through the desert, hallucinations of food began to **tantalize** me.
   a. repel   b. cool   c. warm   d. attract

3. The spaceship vanished into the **abyss** of space and was never seen again.
   a. obstacle   b. planet   c. void   d. cloud

4. The spare bedroom became a **vestibule** from which the children could enter another world.
   a. vehicle   b. lobby   c. office   d. utensil

5. The aliens' ability to instantly heal wounds remains an **enigma** to scientists.
   a. solution   b. answer   c. puzzle   d. fact

6. Each night as Shawn watches the stars, he studies how his favorite **constellations** move across the sky.
   a. clouds   b. kites   c. pyramids   d. arrangements

7. Only in science fiction have astronauts traveled far into space to the edge of our **galaxy**.
   a. the Milky Way   b. Earth's orbit   c. the Moon   d. Orion

8. Astronomers and science fiction lovers both use **telescopes** to view and study objects in distant space.
   a. books   b. rockets   c. magnifiers   d. radios

9. Scientists may **conjecture** about intelligent life on other planets, but they have no proof as yet.
   a. speculate   b. plan   c. confirm   d. debate

10. The time travelers **lurked** among the ruins, waiting for a chance to capture the unsuspecting twentieth-century humans.
    a. hid   b. stood openly   c. wandered   d. climbed

Vocabulary Power *continued*

EXERCISE B   Clues Matching

Write the vocabulary word that best matches the clue.

1. The entrance to the school is one. _____

2. The Big Dipper is one. _____

3. Our country's ambassador to France is one. _____

4. You can use this to see things far away. _____

5. The fragrance of fresh-baked bread may do this to you. _____

6. A problem you cannot solve is often one of these. _____

7. Sometimes the dark seems like a giant one of these. _____

8. Burglars do this around buildings before breaking in. _____

9. When you make a guess, you do this. _____

10. It takes many solar systems to make one of these. _____

EXERCISE C   Sentence Completion

Draw a line through the word that *cannot* be used to complete the sentence.

1. Jon is afraid to go to the basement because he thinks monsters are (lurking, collapsing, hiding) in the dark corners.

2. People of ancient times named the (constellations, stars, telescopes) they saw in the sky each night.

3. The ship's (vestibule, entranceway, wing) was enlarged so that several robots could enter at once.

4. As I lay in my bed last night, I was visited by an (emissary, agent, adverb) from another planet.

5. We held hands tightly as we jumped into the unknown (void, abyss, garden) of time travel.

6. The message in the flashing lights is a continuing (mystery, enigma, resolution) to me.

7. Science fiction books are filled with (conjectures, theories, facts) about alien life.

8. The possibility of time travel (beckons, tantalizes, repulses) historians and authors alike.

Vocabulary Power

Lesson 44   Words from Technology

Travel to other worlds, whether through science or imagination, requires technology. Technological machines and systems help travelers find their way, store information, and understand their findings. We also need words to describe the technology in our daily lives. Sometimes these words describe new technology. Sometimes they are familiar words used in new ways. The vocabulary words in this lesson derive from or describe technology.

Word List

calculator	laser	robotics	transistor
computer	microwave	software	word processor
diskette	mouse		

EXERCISE A   Context Clues

Choose the vocabulary word that best completes each sentence.

1. Electric machines may have _____ in them that help send electrical signals.

2. _____ ovens cook food by sending short electromagnetic waves through it.

3. Students may be allowed to use a _____ to solve math problems requiring complicated arithmetic.

4. The Political Club uses a _____ program to publish its monthly newsletter, entering and then revising a range of different articles.

5. More and more people use a _____ in their jobs to write letters, organize data, and visit the Internet.

6. A starting collection of computer _____ might include a word processing program and an e-mail program.

7. Using a _____, eye doctors are able to permanently correct some vision problems.

8. The recent surge in science fiction books and films featuring human-like machines has produced work for people who study _____.

9. _____, which were once used to move information from one computer to another, are quickly being replaced by e-mail transfers.

10. If you look in a computer catalog, you can find almost any kind of _____ you like, even one shaped like a real rodent.

Vocabulary Power continued

EXERCISE B   Clues Matching
Write the vocabulary word that best matches each clue.

1. This is a very small disk. _____

2. You can use this to make dinner. _____

3. It stands for light amplification by stimulated emission of radiation. _____

4. If you want to make machines clean up your room, you should study this. _____

5. At the beach, you sometimes see radios that have these inside. _____

6. You'll probably need yours to take your final exam in math. _____

7. Without this, you have to type your computer commands on the keyboard. _____

8. Owning one of these is a requirement for joining the computer club. _____

9. This is a special kind of computer or computer program just for handling text. _____

10. Many popular games are available in this format. _____

EXERCISE C   Sentence Completion
Circle the letter of the word or phrase that best completes each sentence.

1. In a restaurant, you'd use a calculator to _____.
   - **a.** figure out the tip
   - **b.** find the restroom
   - **c.** read the menu
   - **d.** speak to the waiter

2. Software is used to _____.
   - **a.** clean floors
   - **b.** hammer nails
   - **c.** run computers
   - **d.** help young children get to sleep

3. Microwave energy is most often used _____.
   - a. to build houses
   - b. to cook food
   - **c.** on a tennis court
   - **d.** in ceiling tiles

4. A transistor is usually very _____.
   - **a.** dirty
   - **b.** small
   - **c.** large
   - **d.** old

5. A robotics professor lectures about _____.
   - **a.** machines
   - **b.** rowing
   - **c.** painting
   - **d.** ancient rocks

6. An electronic mouse is _____.
   - **a.** a small rodent
   - **b.** a remote control for your television
   - **c.** a neon sign
   - **d.** a device to control your computer

Vocabulary Power

Vocabulary Power

Lesson 45   Prefixes That Tell Where

The prefixes *sub-*, *inter-*, and *mid-* all tell something about location. *Sub-* means "under," *inter-* means "among" or "between," and *mid-* means "middle." You can use these prefixes to help you determine the meaning of words containing them. All the vocabulary words in this lesson begin with *sub-*, *inter-*, or *mid-*.

Word List

intermission	midair	subhuman	subordinate
international	midpoint	submarine	substructure
intersection	midrange		

EXERCISE A   Vocabulary Equations

Complete the vocabulary equations. Then, look up each vocabulary word in a dictionary and write its meaning.

1. *sub + marine* = _____

   Dictionary definition _____

2. *inter + national* = _____

   Dictionary definition _____

3. *mid + point* = _____

   Dictionary definition _____

4. *inter + section* = _____

   Dictionary definition _____

5. *mid + range* = _____

   Dictionary definition _____

6. *inter + mission* = _____

   Dictionary definition _____

7. *sub + human* = _____

   Dictionary definition _____

8. *mid + air* = _____

   Dictionary definition _____

9. *sub + ordinate* = _____

   Dictionary definition _____

10. *sub + structure* = _____

    Dictionary definition _____

Vocabulary Power *continued*

EXERCISE B Definitions

Draw a line through the italicized word or phrase. Above it, write the vocabulary word that can replace the word or phrase.

1. NATO is a(n) *relations between nations* organization that often works together to protect its member nations.

2. We will stop at the *point halfway through* to review our work and take a short break.

3. During World War II, the Germans used *boats that go underwater* to sink many Allied ships and cut off supplies to England.

4. In California, the *part of a structure under other parts of the structure* of tall buildings must be able to withstand earthquake tremors.

5. After you drive ten miles on Route 45, watch carefully for the blinking light at the *point where two parts cross* of Tower Hill Road.

6. Historians have carefully documented the *less than human* behavior of Adolf Hitler and his followers during World War II.

7. It is important for commanding officers to treat their *lower in rank* comrades with respect, despite the officers' superior rank.

8. I will meet you in the lobby during the *break between the main activity* so that we can exchange ideas about the lecture.

9. These weapons are specially designed to hit *medium distance* targets with extremely high accuracy.

10. During target practice, we must shoot at clay pigeons tossed in *the middle of the air* by our instructor.

EXERCISE C Multiple-Meaning Words

Use a dictionary to look up the word *subordinate*. Note that *subordinate* can be either a noun, an adjective, or a verb. Write a sentence for each definition of the word.

Vocabulary Power

Vocabulary Power

Lesson 46   Using Test-Taking Skills
Analogies
One type of question often found on vocabulary tests is the analogy question. Analogies ask you to analyze the relationships between words. For example, how are the words *aloof* and *approachable* related? They are antonyms, words with opposite or nearly opposite meanings. In an analogy test question, you would have to recognize this relationship and choose a second pair of words that reflects the same kind of relationship. Here are some tips to help you answer these types of questions.

> **a.** Create a simple sentence in your mind that states the relationship between the first pair of words.
> **b.** Try each of the answer choices in a similar sentence as part of a second word pair.
> **c.** Rule out words that make no sense in your trial sentences.
> **d.** Consider several common types of analogies such as synonym/antonym, part/whole, example/category, and act/actor.

EXERCISE
Choose the letter of the word that correctly completes each analogy.

1. splice : sever :: hostile : _____
   a. friendly   b. gorgeous   c. furious   d. frightened

2. cutlery : teaspoon :: vehicle : _____
   a. tires   b. garage   c. motorcycle   d. driver

3. student : diploma :: employee : _____
   a. lunchbreak   b. salary   c. office   d. briefcase

4. plausible : possible :: hilarious : _____
   a. miserable   b. comedian   c. joke   d. laughable

5. crevice : mountain :: kitchen : _____
   a. cooking   b. home   c. forest   d. microwave oven

6. husband : spouse :: emerald : _____
   a. jewel   b. ruby   c. jewelry store   d. emerald mine

7. vacate : occupy :: deduct : _____
   a. subtract   b. eliminate   c. increase   d. calculate

8. baseball : football :: Kansas : _____
   a. America   b. Kansas City   c. Canada   d. California

9. beverage : milk :: book : _____
   a. novel   b. library   c. magazine   d. writer

10. erratic : unpredictable :: insolent : _____
    a. courteous   b. unhappy   c. insulting   d. amusing

Vocabulary Power

Review: Unit 12

EXERCISE A

Circle the word in parentheses that best completes the sentence.

1. The accidental sinking of a ship in (midair, international, midpoint) waters nearly caused a war.

2. Different cultures throughout history have named the (robotics, constellations, emissaries) that people see in the sky each night.

3. To use your computer effectively and completely, you need a properly functioning (calculator, telescope, mouse).

4. The school district has sent me as their (emissary, transistor, robot) to suggest a friendly solution to our disagreement.

5. For distance shots, photographers use camera lenses similar to (calculators, telescopes, constellations).

EXERCISE B

For each group of words, circle the letter of the word that fits the clues.

1. chasm, void, gorge
   a. vestibule   b. enigma   c. abyss   d. transistor

2. mystery, puzzle, riddle
   a. emissary   b. abyss   c. vestibule   d. enigma

3. universe, cosmos, solar system
   a. galaxy   b. submarine   c. constellation   d. abyss

4. application, program, network
   a. laser   b. software   c. transistor   d. microwave

5. pause, break, recess
   a. intersection   b. intermission   c. international   d. midrange

6. guess, hypothesis, speculation
   a. enigma   b. conjecture   c. substructure   d. abyss

7. monitor, main frame, hard drive
   a. computer   b. laser   c. microwave   d. robotics

8. light, surgery, tool
   a. laser   b. microwave   c. diskette   d. word processor

9. entry, lobby, foyer
   a. galaxy   b. abyss   c. vestibule   d. midpoint

10. foundation, base, underpinning
    a. submarine   b. intersection   c. substructure   d. subordinate

Vocabulary Power

Test: Unit 12

PART A

Circle the word in parentheses that best completes each sentence.

1. Detective Juarez would (tantalize, lurk, conjecture) in the shadows until he spotted the suspect.

2. Please bring in your (diskette, calculator, telescope) so we can put your article on the school's computer.

3. All hikers will meet at the (intermission, intersection, midair) of the blue and white trails.

4. Without evidence to back it up, your theory is just (enigma, emissary, conjecture).

5. This (software, calculator, mouse) can translate documents into Spanish at the touch of a button.

6. You may use your (diskette, calculator, telescope) during the final exam in algebra.

7. July 1 is the (midrange, midpoint, microwave) of the year.

8. The small (international, intersection, intermission) airport has flights to Canada and Mexico.

9. Ambassador Greene was an (emissary, enigma, abyss) for our country during World War II.

10. If you were my (submarine, subordinate, substructure), you would have to follow my orders.

PART B

Circle the letter of the word or phrase that best completes each sentence.

1. If you are in a vestibule, you're probably _____.

 a. eating dinner
 b. changing your clothes
 c. just entering or leaving someplace
 d. doing laundry

2. A constellation contains _____.

 a. a pattern of stars
 b. text documents
 c. planets and galaxies
 d. electrical transistors

3. You're most likely to find a transistor _____.

 a. on the branch of a tree
 b. staying cool in a refrigerator
 c. inside an electrical device
 d. for sale in an ice cream store

4. When your mouse breaks, it is difficult to use your _____.

 a. television
 b. computer
 c. bicycle
 d. telephone

5. An intermission gives the actors in a play _____.

 a. fame and fortune
 b. a chance to sing
 c. time to make the audience laugh
 d. a brief rest

6. Faced with an enigma, you probably feel _____.

  a. excited

  b. puzzled

  c. angry

  d. frightened

7. If the conditions are subhuman, they are _____.

  a. extremely bad

  b. worth repeating

  c. comfortable

  d. absolutely perfect

8. Laser technology works through _____.

  a. light

  b. water

  c. ice

  d. strength

9. When you tantalize people, they feel _____.

  a. startled

  b. generous

  c. horrified

  d. interested

10. If you're at the edge of the galaxy, you've _____.

  a. been on a boat

  b. taken a long bike ride

  c. traveled through space

  d. just gotten off a helicopter

Vocabulary Power

abate   ə bāt´
abstract   ab´strakt
abyss   ə bis´
access   ak´ses
acclaim   ə klām´
accolade   ak´ə lād´
acquire   ə kwīr´
acronym   ak´rə nim´
adaptable   ə dap´tə bəl
adulation   aj´ə lā´shən
advantageous   ad vən tā´jəs
adversity   ad vur´sə tē
aesthetic   es thət´ik
affectionate   ə fek´shə nit
affirmation   af´ər mā´shən
afflicted   ə flikt´id
affliction   ə flik´shən
ambiguous   am big´ū əs
ambivalence   am biv´ə ləns
amends   ə mendz´
amicable   am´ə kə bəl
amorous   am´ər əs
analogous   ə nal´ə gəs
anarchist   an´ər kist
anecdote   an´ik dōt´
articulate   *adj.*, är tik´yə lit; *v.*, är tik´yə lāt
artifact   är´tə fakt´
aspirant   as´pər ənt
aspiration   as´pə rā´shən
aspire   əs pīr´
astonished   əs ton´ishd
atheist   ā´thē ist
audacious   ô dā´shəs
audible   ô´də bəl
audition   ô dish´ən
autobiography   ô´tə bī og´rə fē
aversion   ə vur´zhən
avocation   av´ə kā´shən
belligerent   bə lij´ər ənt
bemused   bi mūzd´
benediction   ben´ə dik´shən
bereft   bi reft´
bibliography   bib´lē og´rə fē
blighted   blīt´id
brazen   brā´zən
calculator   kal´kyə lā´tər
capacity   kə pas´ə tē
capricious   kə prish´əs
captivity   kap tiv´ə tē
cardiologist   kär dē ol´ə jist
cease   sēs

circuitous   sər kū´ə təs
circulate   sur´kyə lāt´
circumference   sər kum´fər əns
circumstance   sur´kəm stans´
circumvent   sur´kəm vent´
clamor   klam´ər
clearinghouse   klēr´ing hous´
cliche   klē shā´
cloister   klois´tər
close   klōz
comedian   kə mē´dē ən
commandeer   kom´ən dēr´
commemorate   kə mem´ə rāt´
commendable   kə men´də bəl
compassion   kəm pash´ən
computer   kəm pū´tər
concede   kən sēd´
confidential   kon´fə den´shəl
conjecture   kən jek´chər
console   kon sōl´
conspiracy   kən spir´ə sē
conspirator   kən spir´ə tər
conspire   kən spīr´
constellation   kon´stə lā´shən
constricting   kən strikt´ing
contemptible   kən temp´tə bəl
contradict   kon´trə dikt´
controversy   kon´trə vur´sē
conventional   kən ven´shən əl
conviction   kən vik´shən
convivial   kən viv´ē əl
coordination   kō ôr´də nā´shən
credible   kred´ə bəl
creed   krēd
cross-examine   krôs´ig zam´in
crucial   krōō´shəl
crucifix   krōō´sə fiks´
crucifixion   krōō´sə fik´shən
cruciform   krōō´sə fôrm´
crucify   krōō´sə fī´
cruise   krōōz
cruiser   krōō´zər
crusade   krōō sād´
crux   kruks
debilitate   di bil´ə tāt´
dedicate   ded´ə kāt´
defensible   di fen´sə bəl
deferential   def´ə ren´shəl
defiant   di fī´ənt
deplorable   di plôr´ə bəl
deplore   di plôr´

depress   di pres´
despicable   des´pi kə bəl
detached   di tacht´
dictator   dik´tā´tər
diction   dik´shən
dire   dīr
disconsolate   dis kon´sə lit
disembark   dis´im bärk´
disingenuous   dis´in jen´ū əs
diskette   dis ket´
disparage   dis par´ij
diverse   di vurs´
dolphin   dol´fin
dote   dōt
double talk   dub´əl tôk´
dovetail   duv´tāl´
dubious   dōō´bē əs
ebb   eb
ecstasy   ek´stə sē
edification   ed´ə fi kā´shən
editorial   ed´ə tôr´ē əl
effervescent   ef´ər ves´ənt
elated   i lā´tid
emissary   em´ə ser´ē
emotion   i mō´shən
empathy   em´pə thē
enclosure   en klō´zhər
encore   äng´kôr
endeavor   en dev´ər
enigma   i nig´mə
enterprise   en´tər prīz´
ephemeral   i fem´ər əl
epiphany   i pif´ə nē
epitaph   ep´ə taf´
eulogy   ū´lə jē
evident   ev´ə dənt
exceed   ik sēd´
excess   ek´ses
exclude   iks klōōd´
exclusion   iks klōō´zhən
excruciating   iks krōō´shē ā´ting
exorbitant   ig zôr´bə tənt
expanse   iks pans´
expatriate   eks pā´trē āt´
expediency   iks pē´dē ən sē
expiration   eks´pə rā´shən
expire   iks pīr´
extract   iks trakt´
extraneous   eks trā´nē əs
extricate   eks´trə kāt´
extrovert   eks´trə vurt´

exuberance   ig zōō´bər əns
exult   ig zult´
face   fās
fallible   fal´ə bəl
falter   fôl´tər
fervent   fur´vənt
fiasco   fē as´kō
fiddle   fid´əl
forgery   fôr´jər ē
fortitude   fôr´tə tōōd´
fortuitous   fôr tōō´ə təs
fretful   fret´fəl
fugitive   fū´jə tiv
galaxy   gal´ək sē
gall   gôl
garb   gärb
generous   jen´ər əs
genial   jēn´yəl
genuine   jen´ū in
giraffe   jə raf´
gratitude   grat´ə tōōd´
gregarious   gri gār´ē əs
habitat   hab´ə tat´
halfway house   haf´wā´hous´
harmonious   här mō´nē əs
highbrow   hī´brou´
hospitality   hos´pə tal´ə tē
hydrant   hī´drənt
hydrate   hī´drāt
hydraulic   hī drô´lik
hydrogen   hī´drə jən
hydrography   hī drog´rə fē
hydrophobia   hī´drə fō´bē ə
hydroplane   hī´drə plān´
hydrosphere   hī´drə sfēr´
hydrotherapy   hī´drō ther´ə pē
hydrothermal   hī drō thər´məl
idolize   īd´əl īz´
illegible   i lej´ə bəl
illustrious   i lus´trē əs
immaterial   im´ə tēr´ē əl
immortality   im´ôr tal´ə tē
impaired   im pārd´
impartial   im pär´shəl
impassive   im pas´iv
impassively   im pas´iv lē
impenitent   im pen´ə tənt
imperceptible   im´pər sep´tə bəl
impersonate   im pur´sə nāt´
imperturbable   im´pər tur´bə bəl
impervious   im pur´vē əs

implausible im plô′zə bəl
imposing im pō′zing
imprint im′print′
imprison im priz′ən
incomprehensible in′kom pri hen′sə bəl
indispensable in′dis pen′sə bəl
inertia i nur′shə
infallible in fal′ə bəl
insatiable in sā′shə bəl
intermission in′tər mish′ən
international in′tər nash′ən əl
intersection in′tər sek′shən
intractable in trak′tə bəl
introspection in′trə spek′shən
intuition in′tōō ish′ən
irascible i ras′sə bəl
irate ī rāt′
irresolute i rez′ə lōōt′
irresponsible ir′i spon′sə bəl
irreverent i rev′ər ənt
jeopardy jep′ər dē
jostle jos′əl
kayak kī′ak
laden lād′ən
lament lə ment′
landmark land′märk′
languor lang′gər
larder lär′dər
laser lā′zər
lavish lav′ish
legacy leg′ə sē
limousine lim′ə zēn′
longevity lon jev′ə tē
lurk lurk
lyrics lir′iks
majestic mə jes′tik
malapropisms mal′ə prop iz′əms
malevolent mə lev′ə lənt
malicious mə lish′əs
malodorous mal ō′dər əs
manuscript man′yə skript′
martial mär′shəl
maternal mə turn′əl
melancholy mel′ən kol′ē
microwave mī′krə wāv′
midair mid′âr′
midpoint mid′point′
midrange mid′rānj′
midseason mid sē′zən
midsection mid sek′shən
midyear mid′yēr′

mile mīl
milestone mīl′stōn′
millefleurs mil flər′
millennium mi len′ē əm
milligram mil′ə gram′
milliliter mil′ə lē′tər
millimeter mil′ə mē′tər
millionaire mil′yə nār′
millipede mil′ə pēd′
millisecond mil′ə sek′ənd
mobilize mō′bə līz′
monogram mon′ə gram′
mortality môr tal′ə tē
mouse mous
multitude mul′tə tōōd′
nationality nash′ə nal′ə tē
nautical nô′ti kəl
nonconformist non′kən fôr′mist
nostalgia nos tal′jə
notable nō′tə bəl
novelty nov′əl tē
object ob′jikt
off-putting ôf′poot ting
ominous om′ə nəs
onomatopoeia on′ə mat′ə pē′ə
optimist op′tə mist
optimistic op′tə mis′tik
optional op′shən əl
orator ôr′ə tər
originate ə rij′ə nāt′
ornate ôr nāt′
overblown ō′vər blōn′
over-the-counter ō′vər thə koun′tər
paleontologist pā′lē on tol′ə jist
parallel par′ə ləl′
paramount par′ə mount′
persevere pur′sə vēr′
perspiration pur′spə rā′shən
perspire pər spīr′
plagiarist plā′jə rist
pliable plī′ə bəl
postdate pōst′dāt′
postmortem pōst′môr′təm
postscript pōst′skript′
postseason pōst sē′zən
posttest pōst′test
potato pə tā′tō
potent pōt′ənt
pragmatist prag′mə tist
precaution pri kô′shən
preclude pri klōōd′

precocious   pri kō´shəs
predator   pred´ə tər
predetermined   prē´di tur´mind
predictable   pri dikt´ə bəl
preface   pref´is
prehistoric   prē´his tôr´ik
pressure   presh´ər
prestigious   pres tēj´əs
privation   prī vā´shən
proceed   prə sēd´
process   pros´es
proclamation   prok´lə mā´shən
profound   prə found´
propagandist   prop´ə gan´dist
prophetic   prə fet´ik
provident   prov´ə dənt
provisional   prə vizh´ən əl
quarry   kwôr´ē
quay   kē
quest   kwest
realize   rē´ə līz´
recede   ri sēd´
recess   rē´ses
recognize   rek´əg nīz´
reflective   ri flek´tiv
refugee   ref´ū jē´
reluctance   ri luk´təns
reminiscent   rem´ə nis´ənt
renaissance   ren´ə säns´
rendezvous   rän´də vōō´
repertory   rep´ər tôr´ē
reproach   ri prōch´
repulsive   ri pul´siv
resilient   ri zil´yənt
resourceful   ri sôrs´fəl
restrict   ri strikt´
reverence   rev´ər əns
revitalizing   ri vī´təl īz ing
revival   ri vī´vəl
revived   ri vīvd
robotics   rō bot´iks
royalist   roi´ə list
ruefully   rōō´fəl lē
sage   sāj
savor   sā´vər
scrupulous   scrōō´pyə ləs
secede   si sēd´
seismologist   sīz mol´ə jist
separatist   sep´ər ə tist
serene   sə rēn´
serenity   sə ren´ə tē

software   sôft´wār´
solace   sol´is
speculate   spek´yə lāt´
squeamish   skwē´mish
stalwart   stôl´wərt
status   stā´təs
steadfast   sted´fast´
stoicism   stō´ə siz´əm
stopgap   stop´gap´
strain   strān
strategy   strat ə´jē
stricture   strik´chər
subdue   səb dōō´
subhuman   sub hū´mən
submarine   sub´mə rēn´
subordinate   sə bôr´də nit
substructure   sub´struk´chər
succeed   sək sēd´
supervise   sōō´pər vīz´
surpass   sər pas´
survivor   sər vī´vər
suspicious   sə spish´əs
sustenance   sus´tə nəns
tantalize   tant´əl īz´
telescope   tel´ə skōp´
tempestuous   tem pes´chōō əs
tenacious   ti nā´shəs
tentatively   ten´tə tiv lē
timorous   tim´ər əs
transaction   tran sak´shən
transcontinental   trans´kon tə nent´əl
transcribe   tran skrīb´
transistor   tran zis´tər
transit   tran´sit
transmission   trans mish´ən
transparent   trans pār´ənt
transplant   trans plant´
trepidation   trep´ə dā´shən
tripod   trī´pod´
tumult   tōō´məlt
turbulent   tur´byə lənt
ubiquitous   ū bik´wə təs
undaunted   un dôn´tid
unkempt   un kempt´
unorthodox   un ôr´thə doks´
unpretentious   un´pri ten´shəs
unsavory   un sā´vər ē
unscrupulous   un skrōō pyə ləs
unwieldy   un wēl´dē
vanquish   vang´kwish
vengeful   venj´fəl

verdict vur′dikt
vestibule ves′tə būl′
vibrant vī′brənt
video vid′ē ō′
vigorous vig′ər əs
visage viz′ij
visible viz′ə bəl
vision vizh′ən
visitation viz′i tā′shən
vista vis′tə
visualize vizh′o͞o ə līz′
vital vīt′əl
vitality vī tal′ə tē
vitalize vīt′əl īz′
vitamin vī′tə min
vivacious vi vā′shəs
vividly viv′id lē
volatile vol′ə til
vulnerable vul′nər ə bəl
wane wān
watchful woch′fəl
wily wī′lē
word processor wurd′ pros′es ər
zealous zel′əs
zoology zō ol′ə jē